The Ancient Aztecs

ALSO BY JESSE J. DOSSICK

Doctoral Research on Russia and the Soviet Union, 1875-1960

Doctoral Research on Russia and the Soviet Union, 1960-1975

Doctoral Research on Puerto Rico and Puerto Ricans

Doctoral Research on Canada and Canadians, 1884-1983

Doctoral Research at the School Of Education, New York University, 1890-1970

Cuba, Cubans, and Cuban-Americans, 1902-1991

History and Guide to Mexico, Vol 1

Mexicana Review: A Journal devoted to the publication of bibliographical as well as popular and scholarly articles on all aspects of Mexicana, Vols. 1-4

The Ancient Aztecs

✦

A complete account of the life of the ancient Aztecs from birth to death

Jesse J. Dossick

Professor Emeritus,
New York University

iUniverse, Inc.
New York Lincoln Shanghai

The Ancient Aztecs

A complete account of the life of the ancient Aztecs from birth to death

iUniverse books may be ordered through booksellers or by contacting:

iUniverse
2021 Pine Lake Road, Suite 100
Lincoln, NE 68512
www.iuniverse.com
1-800-Authors (1-800-288-4677)

Because of the dynamic nature of the Internet, any Web addresses or links contained in this book may have changed since publication and may no longer be valid.

The views expressed in this work are solely those of the author and do not necessarily reflect the views of the publisher, and the publisher hereby disclaims any responsibility for them.

ISBN: 978-0-595-48909-1 (pbk)
ISBN: 978-0-595-48908-4 (cloth)
ISBN: 978-0-595-60892-8 (ebk)

Printed in the United States of America

For Philip and Jane, Joanna and Jeff, Stephen and Carrie, and my Rose

Contents

1

Historical Background and Social Organization

In the fateful year of 1519, bearded men came from the East in small caravels. Armed with fierce weaponry, they plunged the throne of Montezuma into the lake of Mexico, and with it, the civilization of Anahuac.

The fall of this Aztec civilization before the Spanish Conquistadors resulted in the loss of its art, its religion, its social structure, and its language—all that a people must maintain if they are to attain a racial destiny.

The development of the arts and sciences, and the growth of the communities of the ancient Mexican empire came to an abrupt halt; and then began the gradual sinking and disintegration of a great people which lasted four centuries.

It would be difficult indeed to find in history a more convincing example of the complete disaster that might befall a people when stripped of its native culture.

The complex culture of the Valley of Mexico which the Spaniards found, did not, however, originate with the Aztecs. Just as the Romans after their conquest of Greece became submissive to Hellenic civilization, so successive migratory waves of Nahuan nomads from the North, while retaining their crudeness, had conquered the Toltecs, original inhabitants of the Valley.

The name Toltec was used by the Aztecs to describe their predecessors, the supposed builders of a high civilization—Mexico's Golden Age. The word itself means "skilled worker," and was applied by the Aztecs because of their legendary skill as workers of turquoise and jade mosaics, and decorated feather work.

The early history of these migratory tribes is not easy to ascertain in full from the tangled mass of migration myths which have come down to us. These accounts relate that the invading hunters were practically a barbarous people, but modern archaeologists assign to them a fair degree of culture.

1

After a period of settlement, they devoted themselves to agriculture and the arts and crafts, and found themselves adopting the ideas and customs of the Toltecs, being influenced greatly by the superior attainments of the latter's higher civilization. They did more than acquire culture, however, for they actively modified, interpreted, and added to it.

The Aztecs, who similarly were to borrow every feature of the daily life of the Toltecs and their achievements in cultural lines, were the last of the invading Nahuan tribes to reach the valley of Mexico. According to their traditions, they left their mystical home in Aztlan in the north in the latter part of the twelfth century.

Perhaps a hundred years later, after their departure from the north, they arrived at the Mexican plateau, and after some fighting for the right to remain, proceeded to lay the foundations of their new and permanent home on some isolated, unwanted patches of dry land encompassed by the swamps and marshes around the lake of Mexico.

From this date, circa a.d.1325, their historical period may be said to begin, since their accounts, from then up to the Conquest, are fairly definite and reliable.

For a number of years, the Aztecs were comparatively unimportant as a people, lacking in power, and exercising very little influence in the vicinity. Their city, located partly on small islands in the middle of the salt-water lake and partly on newly constructed land in between piles driven into the bottom of the lake, was to prove, however, an ideal defensive site.

During the early years of occupation, the central part of the city was on dry land, industriously reclaimed, while the outlying dwellings stood on piles in the water. Canals, traversing the city, crossed by bridges, ran into causeways at different places.

The construction of the causeways which connected the city with the mainland, and were protected by means of drawbridges, plus the reclamation of the land, were their first major achievements. Their position was admittedly weak, and their attempts to strengthen it resulted in making a stronghold of their settlement.

Early in the fifteenth century, nearly one hundred years after the founding of Tenochtitlan, the Aztecs broke loose from their subjugation to surrounding tribes, and formed an offensive and defensive alliance with two neighboring and kindred groups at Tezcuco, (the Acolhua branch of the Nahuan), and Tlacopan. Of the spoils and tribute, the Tezcucans and Aztecs received two-fifths each, and Tlacopan the remainder.

Within a comparatively short time, the Aztecs converted their defensive stronghold into the most powerful one ever held by Indians up to the sixteenth century, and this very impregnability of Tenochtitlan was an important contributing factor in their rise to power. The Aztecs, thus, from their very modest beginnings, gradually expanded in size (their possession of land), in numbers, and preeminence until their dominating influence came to be felt throughout the greater part of Mexico.

Their first regular war-chieftain, Acampichtli, was elected fifty years after the foundation of Tenochtitlan, and ruled from 1375 to 1396 A.D. It was during 1396 to 1417, however, under Huitzilhuitl, the second ruler, that the wars got under way which gradually succeeded in winning for the Aztecs top ranking among the ancient peoples of Mexico.

By clever political tactics, the Aztecs gradually assumed the paramount position in the confederacy, supreme in war and government. Tezcuco, under the encouragement and sagacious rule of Netzahualcoyotl, (1431-1472), became the intellectual and artistic center of the Valley and maintained her hold upon the cultural ascendancy until the Spanish Conquest. The third member, Tlacopan, gradually became much reduced in importance.

The "empire" of the Aztecs consisted of only a small part of the extensive territories which make up Mexico today. Its boundaries cannot be determined with certainty, although it is believed that at the height of Aztec supremacy, the area controlled or effectively influenced by them extended northward through the highlands of Northern Mexico, eastward to Vera Cruz and Tampico, southward to the distant regions of Chiapes and Yucatan, even to Tehuantepec and far-off Guatemala and Nicaragua, and westward to the Pacific.

No efforts were made by the Aztecs to weld the neighboring tribes who gave momentary and reluctant fealty into a solid commonwealth. They preferred to leave them very much to their old customs, devices, and social and religious organizations, provided the payment of tribute was punctual.

More is known, concerning the social and political organization of the Aztecs, whose largest city was Tenochtitlan, an administrative, military, religious and commercial center of perhaps 200,000 inhabitants, the magnificent "city of palaces," the city of stone and adobe houses, of great public buildings and pyramids and temples and bridges and aqueducts and canals and causeways, than any of the more enlightened Indians of Mexico, because the early Spanish friars and historians studied them more adequately than they did any of the other groups.

In addition, the Aztecs unquestionably had a substantial influence upon the social and political life of the lesser civilized people of Mexico. The Aztecs were then among the best representatives of early Mexican culture.

At the time of the Conquest, the Aztec nation's government was in the form of something approximating an elective monarchy. Functionaries concerned with civil and military affairs were set apart, but because military service was obligatory for all, the establishment of a military caste in its true meaning, had still been prevented.

Economic organization can be said to have been more communistic than socialistic, though it seems that there was a drift in the direction of the formation of an aristocracy through the enrichment and aggrandizement of certain families.

Descent, as might be expected among an agricultural people, was through the father, succeeding the matrilineal form customary in the more unsettled nomadic type of society.

It is quite probable that the state was derived from a number of original exogamous clans in which inheritance was through the mother, but by the time of the coming of the Spaniards, the clan was functioning more as a geographical organization than one established on kinship, and the inheritance had reverted from the matriarchal back to the patriarchal form. The certainty that these were exogamous kindred groups, however, has not been established.

The land was shared by three groups of owners. Foremost in importance were the calpulli, or geographical clan, of which there were twenty in existence in Tenochtitlan at the time of the conquest. Each calpulli was in possession of a rather large amount of land in its community. A portion of this land was set aside and tilled jointly by all the men of the calpulli strong enough to labor, for special public purposes: to furnish tribute, military supplies, the maintenance of the temples, the sacerdotal order and religious services, the local chieftains, and lastly, for the entertainment of official visitors.

The second group of land owners was composed of members of the "nobility," the greater part, presumably, of Toltec origin, and kin of the chieftains of the various communities who, for valuable services rendered to the state, were the recipients of private land grants.

These estates usually passed from father to son like the communally owned calpulli lands, but had the advantage of being able to be sold to others of their class but no one else. It seems also, that the nearby peasants were bound to offer aid during harvest time.

The warrior group comprised the last of the landowners, and most of their possessions were located in conquered territory. It was the practice of the Aztecs to make grants of certain parts of the conquered land to warriors who had distinguished themselves noticeably in wars that eventuated in the addition of new territory into the Aztec realm.

Not only were these grants a recompense for bravery, they were also made as steps in the pacification of the new territories, and led to the establishment of patriotic Aztec units which would watch for and take precautions against discontent and disloyalty. In this category too, estates could pass from father to son, but were not transferable, since title was held by the Aztec tribal rulers.

One can safely assume that the vanquished peoples of the region provided the necessary help to maintain these estates.

Each calpulli, although under the supreme rule of the state seems to have possessed a certain amount of autonomy in governmental matters. In addition, each had a local religious organization with its own god, and central place of worship.

Of the elected officials of the calpulli, two stand out as being the most important, and were known as calpullec. The first acted as the military chief of the group, for each calpulli went forth to war as a unit. Added to his military duties was the responsibility of teaching the young men of the division warlike exercises, and the performance of ceremonial functions.

The second, acting in a civil capacity, seemed to have included among his duties the disposal of the agricultural products of the calpulli land worked jointly for religious and civil needs.

The chief, at the head of each of the four large divisions, was also elected, and was of a very high military rank. Their duties included (in addition to being the immediate military assistants to the war-lords of the tribe), the supervision of their respective quarters for the maintaining of order, and the carrying out of the judicial decisions of the tribal council.

The sharp distinctions and degrees of rank in the social organization of the Aztecs was strongly expressed in externals such as articles of clothing, ornaments of every kind, and in war costumes and insignia of military rank. The classes belonging to the higher scale of their society wore more elaborate and costly costumes, also having the exclusive right to wear certain insignia as shoulder coverings and loin cloths with certain designs which indicated their different military, political and hierarchical degrees.

As evidence of their high rank, we find that in their dress these four war-lords were permitted to tie their hair with red leather, a privilege reserved only for that of the tribal war chief and the Snake-woman, (someone aptly named to symbolize the goddess of motherhood and fertility, yet a post held always by a man).

Above them, and highest in rank, stood the war chief of the state. Early Spanish historians frequently represented Tenochtitlan as the seat of an empire, and described this ruler or war-chief as a person possessing the power of an absolute monarch.

Later writers insisted that the social organization of the Aztecs was virtually democratic. Modern opinion favoring a compromise accepts the midway mark between these extremes. It seems most probable that although succession was not hereditary but elective, selection was limited to a select lineage.

This highest rank was a dual one, however, with a second great chief of similar rank but different duties bearing the title of Snake-woman, or Cihuacohuatl. He appears to have been the executive chieftain for tribal affairs, possibly in control of the war commissariat, and the acquisition and disposal of tribute.

That he was not essentially a civil officer is seen in Cortes' account of the siege of the city by the Conquistadors, for while Montezuma led the combined confederate troops, the Snake-woman was at the head of the local Mexican forces. One of the proofs of the equality of rank between the Tlacatecuhtli and the Snake-woman is that they both enjoyed the same privileges concerning style of dress, insignia (wearing of the copilli or royal crown), and the same burial rites.

While the equality of the Snake-woman to the military ruler is recognized in name, there is some doubt as to whether he was in reality as powerful. The combined leadership of the Aztec tribe was thus in the hands of the two executives plus the tribal council.

The most learned and one of the most powerful groups in Aztec society were the priests. It seems that the religious activities of the Aztecs, originally a simple native worship, were led under the guidance of the clan leaders. Later however, as their civilization advanced, these activities became correspondingly complex as we shall see in our discussion of their religion and education.

A resulting elaboration of ritual radically changed the former simple nature worship into a complex theology which continued to be under the guidance of the clan leaders who now often, also became priests. It was not unusual therefore, for political and religious functions to become closely linked, interwoven, and correlated, since the leaders of the clans were performing the respective duties of each.

As a result, a true theocracy rule by the gods with the priest chiefs as intermediaries, became the outcome of such a social arrangement, and the tribal policy came to be dictated almost as much by religious as by political considerations.

There was also an official group ranking as warriors and "nobles," and members of an order of merit, the Tecuhtlis, entrance to which was granted for conspicuous valor. As the tribe increased in size and power, it became impossible for the Chieftain to assume all of his responsibilities such as exercising justice, regulating the joint affairs of the tribe, waging wars, and to perform also the priestly duties which belonged to him as head of the tribe.

The overflow of royal duties then were apportioned to a caste of lesser chieftains which grew up with him. Called by the general name "tecuhtli" or prince, these men served as officers of justice, managers, and military chieftains, for whom a series of special titles were given, and who were subdivided many times according to their rank.

The rank was assigned by the ruler as well as the benefit of certain tenures which were associated with the various positions. These privileges however were granted only to the "tecuhtli" for the duration of his lifetime. At death, they reverted to the tribal chieftain.

No definite taxes were forthcoming from them, but those personal services, which took the form of holding positions, usually military in origin, and acting as part of the ruler's retinue, were considered payment in kind.

In the social ranking, we next find the highly esteemed and influential merchants, and skilled craftsmen who were both organized in bodies, and exempt from personal services, save for the most urgent cases.

Under them, were the peasants who had a share in the communal calpulli land, and the teccales who also occupied land belonging to the community but who had the added responsibility of working for the noblemen of the neighboring establishments.

At the bottom of the scale were two unprivileged groups: one that might be described as a property less free man, and the other, the slaves. The first was composed in part of expropriated aliens, and of others who had lost their right to clan membership for reasons such as declining to marry, or to farm or cultivate their lands.

These eked out their existence in the face of heavy taxes and services, working either as porters or as serf-like tenants attached to certain fields of the lords, and the gradually greatly extended temple lands for the support of the very considerable sacerdotal class.

All things considered, slavery was a rather benign institution among the Aztecs, not at all like the brutal and inhuman enslavement of people as we have come to understand the term.

The slave class found its ranks filled from various sources. Spendthrifts, wastrels, drunks, gamblers, etc. unable to pay their debts, were obliged to become slaves. Also, children sold by parents in acute need, boys and girls advanced as part of the tribute of the people of conquered tribes, criminals of certain characteristics, and unfortunates among the property less, selling themselves freely, became recruits.

With the military ascendancy of the Aztecs, there came about a corresponding rise to supreme importance of the warrior group. One of the first indications of the change in their social structure became apparent in the distribution of new lands to the men who fought battles, resulting in a perceivable inequality in the size of individual possessions.

This led quite naturally to the development of more conspicuous discriminations between the large landowners and the remainder of the tribe.

When Montezuma II was elected tribal chief after the death of his father, Ahuitzol, in 1502, the first official recognition of class differences appeared, when the former ordered the dismissal from all positions of importance of all those who were not of the ruling caste.

It is evident, therefore, that the Aztecs were passing through a transitional stage, evolving from a loose democratic federation of clans, into something approaching a militaristic aristocracy, which was slowly grasping all control from the clans.

2

Aztecs at Birth

The social fabric of a nation is not revealed in its doctrines and theories alone, but also in its modes of behavior and practical institutions. Turning to primitive peoples, we perceive in the large mass of facts dealing with their daily lives a social and religious etiquette which is adhered to in the several crises of life, such as baptism, marriage, and death, and all are practices which have been found to be common among many peoples throughout the world.

The ancient Mexicans were distinguished by their extreme ceremoniousness on these occasions. Even in their most common relations, public and private, they submitted themselves to certain rules, which made up their code of conduct.

These prescribed rules of action were committed to memory in the temple schools, or in the home, often in the form of speeches, and were repeated in the very same fashion on all identical situations.

These speeches, many of which the early chroniclers have preserved for us, are very often full of religious ideology and references to the gods, and show a sententious language, complete with figures and images, copiously supplied with significant words, and characterized by the utmost refinement.

Education among the Aztecs began at the very moment of a child's entrance into the world, when we observe the ceremonial character of the activities surrounding the event and the inclusion of the other children as active participants, and the esteem with which it was regarded; and when we obtain an insight into the treatment of the enceinte woman, and how she submitted to a kind of material and moral regimentation sanctioned by custom to safeguard the child she is about to bring into the world.

We learn also, incidentally, something of their knowledge of obstetrics, all of which contributes to the appraising of the culture and stage of the Aztecs in their development.

The birth of a baby, especially if it was a son, furnished the motive for many sacrificial ceremonies offered to the gods in behalf of the expectant mother and her child, and for the purpose of rendering certain a happy and brilliant future for the newcomer.

As soon as it was evident to the young married woman that she was to become a mother, she advised her parents, and shortly thereafter a meeting of the husband's and wife's families and relations took place in which many lengthy speeches of mutual felicitation were exchanged.

Typically, this reunion closed with a feast which was repeated when the woman reached the seventh or eighth month of her pregnancy, but on this occasion only the older men and women were present. After the indispensable dinner, they selected a midwife, called "ticitl."

The midwife, in endeavoring to protect the pregnant woman from all physical dangers, set up rules and regulations for safe conduct during pregnancy. She counseled the young wife against overheating herself before the fire, against unnecessarily exposing herself to the rays of the sun, and against sleeping during the day for fear of deforming the face of the child; to partake of sufficient nourishment to be better able to put up with the trials of labor and to be in a position to nurse the child suitably when born.

The young woman was asked not to grieve or to permit herself to become angry nor to expose herself to any fears in order to prevent miscarriage or damage to the baby. The people of the household were warned at the same time to give without any delay all that the mother asked, for fear that the child might otherwise sustain an injury, because of the mother's frustration.

There were also supernatural dangers which surrounded the pregnant woman and for which protective measures had to be taken. She was to abstain from seeing persons put to death—especially by hanging or strangulation—because it was believed that if she did, her child would be born with a cord of flesh around its neck.

Similar superstitions can be found today in all parts of the world. For example, in some eastern European countries, some people believe that if pregnant women wind wool around their necks or wear necklaces, the child will be born with its umbilical chord twisted around its neck.

This belief in maternal impression as a cause of certain congenital abnormalities and deformities has persisted for thousands of years. It was by the maternal impression that ancient medicine and folklore accounted for the occurrence of all kinds of congenital abnormalities, from moles to monsters.

Thus, if the Aztec woman chanced to look upon the sun or the moon at the time of an eclipse, her child would be born with the physical defect of a harelip. If however, the expectant mother placed a small obsidian knife over her bosom, she could regard the phenomenon without fear.

It was believed that if the mother did not follow the midwife's instructions with respect to eating chicle, the child would suffer from shortness of breath and pass away soon after birth.

Another superstition, one connected with the preparation of food, was the belief that if while cooking, a housewife's dinner stuck fast to the pot, she would most likely never bear children; and if somehow she managed to anyway, it would only be with the greatest of difficulty.

Similarly, there existed among the Aztecs a belief in paternal impressions, although it is true that congenital abnormalities were less frequently attributed to the latter than to the maternal impressions. Some of the precautions which were set up for the pregnant woman's guidance were therefore frequently observed by the father too, for the purpose of safeguarding the child from any evil consequences of undue paternal indulgences.

If the father was used to taking walks after sundown, and thought he saw "phantoms," the child would be born with a weak heart. The man could avoid this by taking with him some pebbles, or leaves of wild tobacco.

Sexual intercourse with the husband was encouraged during the first trimester of the wife's pregnancy, though of course with moderation, because it was believed that complete abstinence would result in the child being born sickly and without strength. The act was forbidden, however, after that three month term.

Further, the woman was advised to eat well, to be free of much physical activity, to maintain peace of mind and spirit, and to be employed only moderately in manual labor.

The steam-bath, or temazcalli, was frequently administered by the midwife to the pregnant woman during the last three months, and was a significant practice in relieving the mother of pain, and helping delivery. The midwife carefully avoided making the steam-bath too hot for fear that mother and child could be roasted. The steam-bath was common in Middle American regions, but that of the ancient Aztecs was often more advanced than that of the other peoples of the Americas.

The "temazcalli" as seen in the codices and described by earlier historians was a rectangular stone structure with a low door having openings for ventilation. Set against one end was a rounded oven with a smoke hole in its summit, a fire door, and an enclosed passage leading into the adjoining compartment.

These semi-sacred edifices, comparable to the Russian baths, were public and free, although those wishing to make use of them often brought a small gift of wood or other material, as a token.

As a curative agent, these temazcalli were held in the highest esteem by the ancient Aztecs, and were especially consecrated, to the "mother of the gods," who it was believed bestowed curative and life-giving powers to the temazcalli, the place where she sees secret things, rectifies what has been deranged in human bodies, and otherwise aids and cures.

It was the custom for pregnant mothers to resort to these baths under the watchful eye of the resident medicine woman, who exhorted her patient on entering, with the words, "Enter into this place, my daughter; enter into the bosom of our Mother, whose name is Yoalticitli, and warm yourself in these baths, the house of flowers of our god."

An intelligent use of massage by the midwife accompanied the bath. The custom and use of the temazcalli has persisted throughout the centuries and can be found throughout Mexico and the world today.

A study of the Mexican codices reveals more concerning obstetrics than any other aspect of Aztec medical science. The codices are graphic with depictions of sex and fertility, and contain many visual depictions and presentations.

The ancient Mexicans, like other early peoples, were concerned deeply with fertility, and esteemed and venerated the generative organs. It is easier to portray the act of copulation more strikingly, than the process of ingesting, and the same can be said of labor, lactation, and the washing of a child. It has been astutely observed that a pregnant woman can be portrayed much more unmistakably than a woman with a headache.

The famous figurine of the Nahuan goddess Ixcuina depicts the protectress of pregnant women in the last stages of labor. The goddess is in a crouching position with arms placed toward the rear, hands bearing against her buttocks; jutting from her pudenda are the head and hands of the child.

The statue is excellent in execution, and with noteworthy anatomical precision we see the muscular effort accompanying childbirth, vividly reproduced, with head thrown back, painfully expressive mouth, and wildly distorted facial features.

When the acute pains of labor were evident, the Aztec midwife assisted with abdominal massage, and manual dilation of the vulva, then gave the woman the crushed roots of the chihuapatli plant to drink. This juice had the effect of causing contractions, which expelled the infant.

If the delivery was prolonged, and the pains became violent, the midwife often gave a tincture of pulverized tail of the animal called "tlaquatzin," which was believed to further induce ejection of the fetus. The desire to seek some means of making delivery quickly and easily was key to the midwife's role. Just immediately prior to the baby's coming into life, the midwife made a solemn entreaty to the gods for help and protection.

The priests often did not officiate at the birth of the child, nor at the baptismal rites that followed, although it was a highly religious ceremony. Some priests, however, did go into the woods for fuel, which they blessed, and conveyed on their backs so to heat the bath used by the woman in labor.

As soon as the child was born, the midwife cut the umbilical cord and buried it as soon as was practical.

There were many superstitions concerning the umbilical chord. Among them was the belief that the cord cut should be at least six inches long so that the child would not be born stupid. Further, it should never be cut with steel, but with an implement made of bamboo or obsidian. It was believed that injury inspired by the cut of a steel knife would certainly visit the child. After the chord was cut, it was tied with black thread. Any color other than black was deemed harmful. The midwife usually saved a part of the cord as a cure for many diseases. The baby was then immediately washed by the midwife, as she prayed to Chalchihuitlicue, goddess of water, for its good fortune and happiness.

The midwife's prayer was some variation of the following general exhortation: "May the invisible gods descend upon this water and cleanse thee of every sin and impurity, and free thee from evil fortune. Oh lovely child, the gods have created thee in the highest place of heaven in order to send thee into this world: but know that the life upon which thou art entering is sad, painful, and full of uneasiness and miseries; nor wilt thou be able to eat thy bread without labor; may the gods assist thee in the many adversities that await thee.

After the washing, she put some water in the hollow of her hand and blew it into the mouth and upon the breast and head of the baby while she offered prayer to the creator gods Ometecutli and Omeciuatl.

These so-called creative deities represented the first human couple on Earth, and are seen reclining side by side in all codices, cross legged under a cover, and in a position of procreation. They were understood to be the "great initiators of life" and were comprehended as sending the human soul to occupy the body made by human procreation, giving warmth and breath to the infant before its birth.

The midwife would then raise her voice to a shout like that of a triumphant soldier, to signify to all that the mother had vanquished the difficulties of childbirth with success.

The mother was seen to be a counterpart of the Aztec warrior, since the act of childbirth itself was a brave and noble fight. On the other hand, women who died in childbirth were regarded in the same light as the fallen soldier.

Upon completion of her other accompanying actions, the midwife then handed the baby to the mother to nurse.

Sometime before the second ceremonial washing, which usually took place on the fourth day after birth, and which was like a christening, a priest-astrologer was called upon to make known the child's lot, and aid in its naming. These were derived from the number and sign of the hour of the day in the sacred Tonalmatl, or calendar.

The Aztecs believed that a person would remain under the influence of the particular sign and number date under which he or she was born, for the remainder of his or her life. Certain days were associated with good fortune; others with adversity; still others with indifference.

The Aztec arts of divination seem now to appear rather more a matter of necromancy than of astrology. From the names of the demons (to which the child's birthday was dedicated), they made countless prognostications concerning the destinies the children had to meet with in life. After the eighteen months of the Aztec year were completed, five days remained, which they considered to be unlucky.

It would have been ill-advised to begin any serious tasks, or hold any type of ritual celebration during these days. It was felt that any children born during these five days would of necessity have to suffer numerous misfortunes, their fate being a poor and miserable one indeed. So, if a boy was born during these days, he would be regarded as a "useless man," or "nemoquichtli," and the child was female, it would be called "nenchihautl," or useless woman.

Children born under "indifferent" signs had to be extra careful in doing penance. If their parents took pains in their education, and endowed them with good habits, they might be more likely to be fortunate; but if they were not well educated, they would almost certainly be unlucky or miserable. This, perhaps, could be regarded as recognition of the value of education.

It was possible, in Aztec tradition, to possibly ward off imminent ill-fortune, but the stratagem of postponing the baptism ceremony usually held four days after birth, to some future time when the gods were more likely to look favorably upon the newborn.

It is probable that the parents were kept in the dark as to the exact workings of the machinery of the priesthood, and the latter were therefore reverenced for their powers of prophecy.

If the ancient Mexicans thus believed implicitly that the sign and date of the child's birth in reality did control his or her future destiny, then it was undeniably in the priesthood's power not only to forecast the child's future, but also to bring to bear a beneficial or adverse influence upon it.

On the morning of the fourth day, or the day designated by the priest-astrologer, just before sunrise, a great festival, including a feast, was prepared at which the second baptism took place, a more solemn rite than the first. Relatives, friends and children were invited, and, according to the wealth of the parents, entertainment was provided, and gifts of wearing apparel made to all present.

The actual baptism involved elaborate preparations, (even more elaborate if the child were the son of a warrior. Often, they made him a little bow and four arrows, and a shield.

If the child were a girl, a special dish of beans and toasted corn was prepared, along with several jewels or precious stones, and the instruments for sewing, spinning and weaving.

When all had been made ready, the family relatives and friends were called to the front of the house to wait for the sun to rise. The midwife took the child in her arms, called for a glazed earthen vessel of water, and for the ornaments that had been collected for the ceremony to be placed in a circle around herself and the child.

The midwife then turned to face the west, moistened her fingers in the vessel of water, gave it to the child to taste, saying, "Take this water and be blessed oh my child, take and receive this water of the Lord of the world, which is our life, and is given for the increasing and renewing of our bodies. This heavenly water is to bathe and to purify. I pray that these drops enter freely into your body and dwell there so to vanquish and remove from you all sin and evil given you before our world began."

Then, she bathed the child, and four times lifted it toward the heavens, each time with a different prayer, the last to the sun god: "Lord, Sun and Tlatltecutli who are our father and mother, behold this creature. I offer it to thee, Lord, who art valiant in war. It is thy creature, born to serve thee.

The first prayer was offered to the gods before named, the second to the goddess of water, the third to all the gods together, and the fourth to the sun and earth. The prayer would go something like, "Oh Sun, the father of all things living upon the earth, and our mother Earth, receive this child and protect it as your own."

A male child would receive additional blessings: "So that this child is born for war, may he die in it, defending the honor of the gods; so may he enjoy in heaven the delights which are prepared for all those who sacrifice their lives in so good a cause."

She then put in his little hands the instruments of the warrior art which he was to exercise, the bow, arrow and shield. With a prayer addressed to the protecting gods, she would say something like, "Behold, the tools of war with which thou are served, and in which thou dost delight. Give unto him the gift thou dost give thy soldiers who die in war, and who are there praising thee."

The implication of course was that by becoming a soldier, he would be in a position to die a warrior's death and thus be enabled to qualify for entrance into the warrior's paradise, the Heaven where the Sun lives.

Torch fires of pine were started at the birth of the child, and great care was taken to see that they burned all throughout the first four days, until the termination of the second bathing ceremony. The Aztecs believed that neglect of the fire would carry away good fortune from the child.

If the baby was female, the baptism differed in many respects. Because of Aztec cultural tradition, the midwife's speech might run along this vein: "Oh my beloved mistress, welcome! Much trouble have you caused; you have been sent into this world by your Father, who as a Creator and Savior is present everywhere. You have come onto this earth where your parents live in need and misery—where depressing heat, rough winds, and cutting icy winters are to be found—where there is no joy or recreation—because here is a place of labor and drudgery. We do not know my daughter, whether you will live here long enough even to see your grandparents and make them happy. We do not know anything about your fate in life, nothing about the favor or grace of God which he may have in store for you. Yours is to stay within the house, as the heart does within the body; our Lord enshrines you in this place. Your office is to fetch water, to grind maize in the "metate," to sweat by the embers."

In the same manner as with a male, tiny implements, in this case for weaving, spinning and cooking, were put in the baby's hands, then placed into the glazed earthenware tub. She was also led through the motion of grinding maize for tortillas. After additional prayer, the baby was placed in the mother's arms with words of caution for its care.

When the religious ceremony was concluded, the feast and entertainment began, the quality and distinction of which corresponded to the rank of the father.

Stillborn children were not unknown to the Aztecs. If the midwife discovered that the unborn child had already died in the womb of the mother, she put her hand into the mother's vagina and cut off the dead baby from the mother with an obsidian knife.

The permission of the parents was needed for this operation, but if they refused it, then the mother was deprived of care, shut up somewhere, and left to die.

Mortality at birth—of children and mother—may have been considerable, for we find constant pessimistic speeches linking the "Hour of Birth" with the "Hour of Death."

The ancient Aztecs felt that a woman who bore the sufferings of childbirth bravely, but who died in the act, deserved therefore to receive the supreme reward of immortality and eternal happiness and entrance into their heavenly paradise. This was an honor granted ordinarily only to the distinguished heroes of the nation, and those who had perished in actual combat on the battlefield.

This linkage to the military in discourse addressed to the woman who had succumbed in childbirth is clear: both midwife and priest would couch their words with tenderness and respect for her exertions.

A typical exhortation might be along the lines of, "Oh my much loved daughter, brave, beautiful and tender dove, thou has exerted thyself and fought as a female warrior; thou has triumphed and acted like thy mother, the Lady Quilaztli. Thou hast fought valiantly. Thou hast used thy sword and shield like a dread and brave warrior, the shield and the sword, which thy mother placed in thy hand.

"Awake therefore, and arise my daughter, for already it is a new day for you, the red has appeared in the sky, already the swallows sing for you. Arise, my daughter and go to that good place, the house of thy father and mother the sun god, where all live in joy and happiness, let thyself be taken there by thy sisters, the celestial women (ciualpipiltin), who live there in glory and in joy."

The ancient Aztecs canonized the "mociuazuetzqui" or women who died in childbirth as goddesses, and worshiped them as such. Their left arms, or the middle finger of their left hand, and even their hair were considered to be sacred talismans to warriors and sorcerers.

Those children that died at birth, however, were believed to go to the home of the god Tonacatecutli. If the death of the child occurred in the first months of life, while the child was still nursing, then it went to the first heavenly residence or children's paradise (called hichihuacuanuhco). Here, it was believed, there was a tree from whose branches milk was secreted, and with it the children nourished themselves. The tree was regarded as the wet-nurse who raised them eternally.

One of the superstitions that was strongly believed by the ancient Aztecs was that the bearing of twins, which occurred frequently, would result in the death of one of the parents. There was only one remedy, and that was to kill one of the twins instead.

Twins were often called "coatl," or serpent, and legend had it that they would devour either father or mother if one of them was not killed. This cruel practice may have come about in a period of tribal history when life was extremely difficult, and parents may have had to literally starve themselves in order to bring up their families.

The historical records of terrible famines which threatened the existence of the nation, as well as innumerable references to the sufferings caused by starvation, give testimony to the fact that far back in their history, before the conquest of the southern provinces with their wealth of foods, vegetables and other food products, the inhabitants of the central plateau of Mexico had frequently to contend with actual starvation.

It is interesting to note that the ancient Aztecs did not have milk-giving domestic animals. As a matter of fact, they possessed no domestic animals other than small dogs and fowl.

All of the children, including those of the royal family, were nourished by their own parents. If the mother was hindered by illness, a nurse was hired, but only when the former was well aware of the latter's condition in life, and the quality of her milk.

Lactation lasted at least two complete years, sometimes even three, for the Aztecs adhered to the doctrine that before this age no substance other than milk ought to occupy the stomach of the baby. In conformity with this, mothers kept to a strict diet that would maintain the quality of their milk. At three years of age, the child began the eating of maize, their staple food.

Some wives deliberately withheld from intercourse with their husbands during this time, to forestall the possibility of another child coming along to interfere with the proper nursing of the first one.

In the fifth month of the Aztec calendar, which was called Toxcatl, and during the first festival of the war god Huitzilopochtli, the priests made a slight wound upon the breast and stomach of all the boys and girls who had been born within the year. This was the token by which the Aztecs acknowledged themselves dedicated to the worship of their protecting war gods.

This act of inflicting slight cuts upon the body of male children in particular, led many early historians to the erroneous belief that rites of circumcision were practiced among the Aztecs. It is generally believed now that this was not the case.

The careful preparation and devotion to these important religious rituals and festivities, and the sharing of these communal experiences made for a closer family kinship. The studying for their roles in the rituals, and the mastery and understanding of hygienic rules mixed with the conscious and unconscious absorption of what we consider to be superstitious beliefs, constituted an important educational process of both a formal and informal nature for all participating, young and old.

3

Early Life of Aztec Children At Home

The human being is not a free agent with reference to culture. He is ushered into the world, sees the light of day, and is reared in some specific cultural environment which has a strong influence upon him at every moment of his life.

From childhood, his behavior is conditioned by the practices of those close to him. He has no other alternative but to accede to the folkways prevailing in his group. We do not have from the ancient Aztecs any works that touch specifically upon education, for as far as we know, their teacher-priests did not put in writing the principles which they followed. A picture of the early training of the children at home, an idea of the moral tendencies and the educational aims and practices of the Aztecs can best be obtained however, from several paintings of that valuable collection called the Mendoza Codex, and from a survey of the daily life and habits of the ancient Mexicans in which the children played a part.

The training of the Aztec child was severe from its very beginning. The directing of the children's education was divided by the parents; the father undertook the training of the boys, and the mothers, the girls. They aimed decidedly to develop their children to become strong, hardened, and dexterous, and physical activities were conducted in keeping with rigid precepts.

From their birth, the children were bathed repeatedly in icy water; they had to sleep in very hard beds, apart from one another; their clothes were few and they went about nearly naked. They were forced to become accustomed to fatigue, something constantly bred within them. This kind of treatment of the children was also practiced by the nobles and the well-to-do, for it was their desire to make their children robust and healthy too.

While the children may have found time for play, games and amusements, still the universal maxim of the elders seems to have been to keep the young boys and girls constantly occupied. Severe punishments were inflicted frequently, for the

20

purpose of preventing any laziness on the part of the children, and to keep them from performing acts of perceived childishness.

In spite of this, Aztec parents demonstrated a tender love for their children. The raising of large families was considered honorable and praiseworthy, and parents were held personally accountable not only for the instruction of their children, but also for their behavior up to the age of entrance into temple schools.

The charge of raising them improperly was deemed an affront which was worse than death, for if a child grew up to be what used to be called a ne'er-do-well, it was said of him mockingly that he had been raised by fools.

When the children reached an early age, usually five or six years, they could be turned over to the priests to be educated in their seminaries. This was generally done by the nobles and wealthier people, but the majority of the children of the middle and lower classes received their elementary training at home from their parents.

One of the precepts most warmly inculcated in youth was truth in their words. Whenever a lie was detected, it was not uncommon for the lip of the delinquent to be pricked with the thorns of the aloe.

Undoubtedly, the Aztecs consciously or unconsciously acknowledged distinct periods in child life and modified training and instruction accordingly. From the Mendoza Codex we learn of the quantity and kind of food which was permitted the children at the various ages; the occupations in which they were employed and instructed, the difficulty of which increased with age; the constant vigilance with which their actions were observed, and the penalties inflicted, the severity of which also kept pace with their age, to rectify wrong doings.

According to the scheme of education as depicted in the Mendoza Codex, we find in the fiftieth painting, a boy of four years whose parents have set him to some difficult tasks for the purpose of hardening him to fatigue, and a mother giving a daughter her first lesson in removing the seeds from cotton. Another boy, of five years, accompanies his father to market, supporting a little bundle on his back, and a girl of the same age begins to acquire a knowledge of spinning.

A boy of six years goes to the market with his father and assists him in picking up the ears of maize which lie scattered on the ground in a square. A mother improves her six year old daughter's handling of the malacatl, or spinning wheel.

The Aztecs, lacking beasts of burden, found it necessary to accustom themselves from early childhood to carry heavy weights on their shoulders; the merchants for their trade; rich and poor for their necessities; soldiers for their arms and baggage. As the children grew older, they carried heavier burdens.

Without the convenience of a means of transportation other than their feet, they also learned to walk great distances, barefoot, through plains and over mountains. Thus, the fundamentals of their education in the early years rested on frugality, work, and the acquisition of strength and endurance, to resist the harsh physical environment.

In the fifty-first painting there is depicted a father who instructs his son of seven years in fishing and construction of nets. It was customary also for the father to teach the son to make fish traps, to show him the best places to put them, to know the names of the different fish in the lake, their habits, and the best ways of catching them. A mother is further improving her daughter's methods of spinning.

Some boys of eight are menaced with punishment if they do not perform their tasks; similarly, the daughter is threatened. A youth of nine years is pierced slightly by his father in several parts of his body in order to correct his unruly temper. A girl of nine years is pricked by the mother, in her hands.

At thirteen years, the boy is instructed by the father to fetch firewood and grass from the fields, and to wield a canoe. The boys were taught to paddle with agility, gracefulness and accuracy, and to master the simple maneuvers of backing water, of steering, and moving paddles in unison with others.

A girl the same age is occupied with domestic duties, and helps the mother grind maize and cook bread. The chief service in which women were employed was cooking. With the Aztecs, this was an especially important occupation, as the chief article of diet, the tortilla, could not be prepared in large quantities to be kept, like bread; it had to be freshly prepared by a somewhat elaborate process for every single meal, and eaten fresh and hot.

The fifty-second painting shows two youths of eleven, who, not having improved after certain punishments, are exposed to the asphyxiating smoke of burning chili or red pepper; a daughter of eleven is exposed to the same punishment by her mother. A boy of twelve is kept for an entire day bound and naked upon a dunghill, as a chastisement by the father for certain faults, and to accustom him to also to hardship; the mother's punishment for a girl the same age is to make her walk sleepless throughout the night in the home and nearby streets.

Further, a youth of fourteen is engaged in receiving instructions from his father in lake fishing. An ideogram of speech in front of the instructor's mouth indicates that verbal instruction was an integral part of this practice, and that all learning was not achieved by imitation alone. In addition to being taught how to catch fish, Aztec youths were instructed in an ingenious method of catching water fowl.

An empty gourd was left to float on the water for a long time, until it was felt that the birds had become accustomed to the sight of it. The hunter would then move in among the birds, quietly, wearing on his head another gourd similar to the empty one, with eye holes punched through however, and with the hands in a free position, ready to snatch his unfortunate prey by its legs under the water.

In every picture, there are drawn some tortillas or cakes of bread to show the amount of food given to the children at different ages. At the age of three, for example, they were allowed only one-half a tortilla for each meal. At four to five, the food ration was increased to one cake of bread. At six or seven, they received one and a half, and this remained so until the age of thirteen.

These few cakes of bread could not possibly have sufficed as nourishment for a daily food ration unless they were unusually large or nutritious. One can intuit that the Codex Mendoza was simply trying to illustrate that although children worked hard, daily, still they were kept to a modest and rigorous diet.

An inspection of the daily life of the Aztecs finds that there was almost no aspect of it, personal or public, in which religion did not play a part. Religious exercises, which included frequent fasting and blood-letting, and numerous sacrifices to the gods, were common, for the people, desiring much from their deities, and fearing them, felt that their fortunes were dependent upon them, and so came to look upon their obligations to them in a matter-of-fact manner.

Activities, such as the meetings of families or calpulli, the reaping of the harvest, changes in the seasons, the birth of a child, rehearsals for war, departure for and return from war, victory, the many festivals of guilds, calpulli, and state, were all occasions for religious ceremonies.

The child, being made conscious of these observances by witnessing them, coming into contact with them by aiding in their preparation, listening to such explanations as parents and elders deemed suitable, received thus his or her early religious training and education.

In reality, the religious education of the child started with the rites of infancy, and as it grew older, its thoughts and conduct were stimulated and guided by these festivals and numerous activities, and words and actions of those around it, until within its consciousness there was gradually built up the religious ideal.

Parents undertook to teach their children modesty of behavior, lessons of proper conduct at home, afield, and at wars, the evils of vice, respect for their gods, and the manner by which they could pray and entreat for their protection and favor. Children were also taken often to the temple, so that they might become attracted to religion.

It is likely that a child's first visit to the temple to witness the service exerted an educative influence upon it as he or she watched with earnestness and awe while the priests moved busily about, making offerings to the gods, of blood, copal, quails, falcons, and other animals.

The calling upon the gods, the bright colors, contagious excitement, the songs and dances of the temple festival, were almost certain to leave a strong impression.

Among the counsels that parents gave their children, the idea that they should be careful about awakening from sleep and keeping vigil; not to sleep all night; not to eat too much in the morning and night; be moderate at dinner and supper; be sure to see to it that breakfast was taken before beginning to work.

In the home, as in the temples, prayer was a prominent and important medium of religious expression. In addition to reenacting in their houses ceremonies modeled after those held in the main temples, the people would pay devotion to their own particular divinity, tribe, or guild. One of the common ceremonies in the Aztec temple involved, on the part of the priest, the taking of some lighted coals from the fire, placing them in a hand censer, then throwing some incense (copal) into it.

The priest then approached the image of the god they were addressing, and raised the censer towards the four cardinal points, separately. Upon completion of these motions, the coals were thrown into the fire.

The same act was imitated by the people in their homes, and parents taught and compelled their children to do the same, every morning and night, to honor, with incense, the images they had in their oratories, or in the yards of the house, wherever the shrine and images were kept.

The children were also compelled to sweep away the dirt (a symbol of sin), with great care, early every morning, from the rooms where the idols stood, as a sign of respect for the gods.

Another of the religious observances taught at an early age to the child was the practice known as the "eating of the earth in honor of the gods." Whenever any woman, man or child entered a building where there were images or idols of the gods, he or she would bend low, and at once touch the earth with his finger tip, then raise it to his tongue and lick it. This act was performed also upon returning home, passing temples or oratories, and as a sign of respect towards a superior.

Even today, when an Indian from the hills makes a pilgrimage to the shrine of Our Lady Of Guadalupe, Mexico's patron saint, it would not be unusual to bow in humiliation as was done centuries ago, and brushing hands across the dusty floor, carry them to his or her lips with the words, "Oh our Mother, I humbly eat this earth in thy presence."

The Aztecs also used this act as a solemn declaration of the truth of a statement, in place of an oath, saying, "By the life of the Sun and of our lady of the Earth, there is no error in my statement, and in proof of this, I eat this earth." The speaker would then stoop and perform the act of carrying the earth to his tongue, and proceed to eat it.

There were several kinds of festivals celebrated in the home, including those which observed some noteworthy occurrences of family life, like birth, baptismal rites, marriage and death rites, all of an intimate nature, and in which the children participated to some extent. There were also the various tribal festival rites which occurred throughout every one of the eighteen months of the Aztec calendar, and which were considered an essential part of their daily life.

Children were by no means excluded. It is open to conjecture whether the original of the festival, and the meaning of each symbolic act was explained to the children, though it is probable that they did so to an extent, in keeping with the latter's age.

Over they years, after making careful study of countless pottery images and heads with the attributes of various divine forms, scholars have advanced the theory that these may have been created for the purpose of giving the images to the children in attendance, to impress the occasion upon their memory.

Another educational significance of the active participation of the children in some of the monthly festivals, was, in addition to bringing them closer to their religion, the fostering of the domination of the ritual upon their lives.

At the festival of Etzalcualiztli, one of the duties of the youths for a certain ceremony consisted of the catching of little birds which were tied by strings to boughs which they then carried while walking in the procession of the festival, the birds all the while fluttering around the boughs. There was another instance at a festival named Panquetzaliztli, in which the boys of the town, aged ten or less, wearing rich mantles, danced around in honor of the idol in the temple square.

The fast of five days before the festival of Mixcoatl, the fast of four days before the festival of Tezcatlipoca, and that which was held previous to the festival of the Sun, all were observed by the children as well as the elders.

According to Aztec belief, the Sun and the world were fated to come to an end on a day called "naui olin," the sign of the present Sun. These ancient Mexicans anticipated the possibility of the world perishing on any of these naui olin days, which recur every two hundred and sixty days. In order to prepare for the event, at each of these days there took place a great four day fast called netonatiuh-caualli, the "Fasting for the Sun," when everyone withdrew to their houses, the kind to a special house called Quauhxicalco.

At noon on each of these four days, the conches were blown, whereupon everyone, great and little, old and young, gashed tongue and ears, and presented the blood to the Sun—doubtless with the intention thereby to give it strength to resume its course for the following year.

Quail and incense were also offered up, and in the temple of Quauhxicalco, four prisoners were sacrificed, two of them being designated as the Chachanme, or "House," and the other two as the "Image of the Sun," and "Image of the Moon." This great fast recurred every two hundred sixty days, and was indelibly associated by all with the motion of the Sun in the heavens.

On the first day of the first month, Atlacahualco, or Qualitocola (correspond-ing to the second day of February), a great festival was held for the gods of rain, called the Tlaloc, at which offerings were made of children, both boys and girls, purchased for sacrifice. Those children only, were selected who had been born on a lucky day, and preferably, had two "crowns" on their heads, or "two grain troughs."

The symbolic interpretation of the latter is understood, when we realize that the radial or spiral arrangement of the hair on the crown of the head was being compared to the high wooden receptacles in which the harvest maize was kept.

Those children with the abnormal two "crowns" on their heads denoted abun-dance of corn. These children, therefore, were the prized offerings, most accept-able to the rain gods, who in turn would cause abundant rain to fall. The children were not all sacrificed immediately, but successively, at subsequent festivals over a period of three months.

At each sacrificial ceremony, the boys and girls were selected in a manner to correspond to the sex of the deity. Two of each sex were drowned in a particular lake at one festival; at a later one, three boys of six or seven years of age were placed in a cavern to die of starvation and terror.

While these sacrifices did arouse feelings of great pity for the children, and caused much weeping on the part of many, they were performed nevertheless, for the purpose of procuring from the gods sufficient rain for the production of maize in the fields. If the children cried on the way, the belief was that this was an omen for copious rains to fall during the planting and harvesting seasons.

Common demands were also made of the youth in all festivals for the perfor-mance of numerous little tasks of religious significance. In addition to catching little birds to be tied to boughs, as mentioned before, the carrying of ears of maize to the temple by virgins to the temple, for offering during the festival of Centeotl, mother of the gods was a usual practice.

These virgins, with arms and legs trimmed with red feathers, were jealously guarded before, during and after the procession, to preserve their status. The ears of maize, becoming hallowed at the temple, were then brought to the granaries, to preserve the remainder of stored grain from mold and deadly insects.

Festivals were also a means of providing the children with recreation. For example, on the tenth day of the eighteenth (last) month or the year, the youth of the calpulli went out on a chase, hunting not only wild game in the woods, but birds of the lake areas. The men and youth formed a great circle, and closed in a great many animals, deer, rabbits, and other game, closing the circle little by little until they had driven them into close quarters and now each could attack and kill what he wanted.

At a festival recurring every fourth year on a fixed day of the eighteenth month called Izcalli, the ears of all children born during the three preceding years were perforated on the lobes, so that they might wear earrings, and a ceremony called "crespa" (i.e. trimming the hair of the children), and teaching them to handle fire, was celebrated. In addition, the high priest perforated the lower lip of the boys so that they could subsequently wear labrets.

The perforating rite was done with a sharp bone instrument, and the wound was quickly dressed with a little oil (ocotzotl) and soft parrot feathers. Previous to the ceremony, the parents of the children sought out godfathers and godmothers to hold the children during the operation. An offering was made of the flour paste made from seeds called chian; then the parents presented the godfathers with a bright red mantle (tilmatl), and the godmothers with a sleeveless upper garment called huipil.

The boys and girls would scream aloud from pain during the ceremony, and afterwards were led by their godparents to a large surrounding fire prepared for the occasion. In the end, they all walked to their respective homes, enjoyed a feast to which the godparents were invited, and danced and sang.

At midday, the children were taken to the temples once again by their godparents who also carried along jugs of pulqe, the native wine. At the temple they would dance, often supporting the children upon their backs, and from time to time would give the latter some pulque to drink in tiny cups, the practice being called the "intoxication of boys and girls."

In addition to their moral and industrial education and their public apprenticeship in the religious festivals, was the teaching of devices by the parents for the warding off of the many evils which surrounded them constantly.

Superstitious observances and habits of a people are learned easiest and accepted quite naturally in childhood, through imitation and instruction around the hearth, and come to constitute a large part of the learning obtained in the home.

We may feel safe in including as part of the education at home the songs and stories of the adventures, calamities, glories and accomplishments of their gods and ancestors, and the experiences of the tribe in former generations.

In addition, there was a type of nature study with the parents drawing upon their legends for explanations of nature's phenomena. For example, in Aztec legend, the moon, was said to have originally shone as brilliantly as the sun, had its features dimmed when the gods flung a white rabbit in its face.

Another told of the humming bird, which was looked upon as the bird of the rainy season. It was said of it that during the dry months, he hung with his bill from a tree, dead and lifeless, dried and featherless. Not until the rainy season started again did he awake to new life, don new feathers, and once again fly from flower to flower.

Superstition provides glimpses of everyday life in the ancient Aztec home. Most of these are concerned with the fireplace, the preparation of food, the bringing up of children, signs by which they could foretell the future, omens, all of which can be considered an integral part of the education of the people.

On the tenth day of the third feast of the year, Tocoztontli, all boys up to twelve years of age were required to draw blood and abstain from food. The wise men, soothsayers and magicians made the rounds of the houses of calpulli, and tied cords of different colors about the necks of these boys who had performed their prescribed penance.

The color of the cords were picked to correspond with the divinity presiding over it. Upon these cords, the magicians placed all kinds of charms, like snake bones, small idols, pebbles strung on strings, which would serve as a protection against diseases.

Prior to any large dinner gathering, the host would bring the image of the god Tezcatlipoca into the house, and there worship and care for it, because if any of his guests found so much as a hair in the soup, or choked in swallowing, it was a sign that the proper honor had not been paid to the god of banquets.

When the building of a new home was completed, the man of the house gathered his family, relatives and neighbors around the new hearth, and attempted to kindle a new fire. If the fire ignited rapidly, it was believed that the new dwelling would be favored by fortune and all would be tranquil.

If the kindling was slow to light, however, then it was believed that the new home would be one of sadness and bad fortune. At this time too, the owner of the new home would prick his ear, secure a drop of blood, place it on the nail of his index finger, and toss the blood, in honor of the god of fire and the sun, into the fire, or in the direction of the sun.

The sacrificial act of drawing blood, mostly from the ear, usually resolved itself into a performance of thanksgiving or repentance, and was a common characteristic of daily life in ancient Mexico, performed by young and old.

This offering to the fire was but a more respectful form of the ceremony called Tlatlacaliztli, which means "the spilling," in furtherance of the idea that nobody should eat without first throwing a small portion of what was going to be eaten into the fire, in honor of the fire god.

Still another general habit was the one of not drinking any wine unless a small quantity has been spilled at the entrance of the house. Whenever they opened a new jug, they would pour a quantity into a glazed earthenware dish and place this near the fire.

From there, they would take it out with a tumbler, pour a cup at the entrance of the house in the four directions (cardinal points of the world), and only after this was done could the guests drink. Before that, no one should dare do so.

Corn cobs were not to be thrown into the fire of a home which had recently been blessed with a new baby, for it was believed that unless precautions were taken, the baby's face would become pitted and pocked like the corn cob itself. The measure to be taken beforehand was the passing of the cobs, before burning, over the face of the child itself.

Persons eating or drinking in the presence of an infant in its cradle were expected to place a bit of their food or drink in its mouth, because it would likely experience fewer hiccups during the course of its life. When a child would lose one of its baby teeth, the father or mother would throw it into a rat-hole, for if this precaution was not taken, the child would never grow another in its place.

Superstitious observances were frequently the means of forcing the children to certain actions which the parents thought were in keeping with good conduct. The threat of the "bogey" man to carry off disobedient children (found in many cultures) was one. These threats were often merely harmless warnings, none of which were calculated to inspire genuine terror.

When an Aztec mother told her son that if he served himself with his hands from the pot containing food for the whole family, or if he dipped sops of bread into it, he would be unlucky in warfare when he grew up, and would probably fall into the hands of his enemies.

It's not hard to imagine that the remoteness of the punishment counteracted the effect of the threat. Its employment however reveals at what an early age the desire for success in warfare was awakened and developed in the minds of the Aztec youth.

Naughty youngsters who licked the metate on which the maize was prepared, were expected to lose their front teeth in short time. Parents discouraged any idleness displayed by their children, as for example, if they found a child leaning against the corner posts, they would restrain him or her, saying, that persons who did so generally became liars, for the posts themselves were thought to be untruthful.

To offset a seemingly common habit on the part of daughters from eating while standing, mothers would pretend that if a girl did so, she would not marry in her village, but elsewhere, far away.

Their recognition of the importance of maize as their staple food was manifested in the obligation on the part of a child (or youth and adult as well), who came across grains of maize which had fallen to the ground, to pick them up as soon as they were seen, for the child was taught that failure to do so would cause offense to the maize, and the maize in turn would complain about the offender to the god of maize, saying words to the effect of, "Lord, punish this person who saw me lying on the ground and did not pick me up; let this person feel the pangs of hunger, so to learn not to despise me."

In the family, age commanded respect, as was demonstrated in the observance of certain etiquette, when brothers or sisters chanced to be drinking together, for if the youngest drank first, the oldest might tell him or her, "Do not drink before me, for if you do, you will not grow any more, but will remain as you are."

Peculiar views concerning the matter of growth were held by the Aztecs. Parents were convinced that any number of different causes or events could be the means of suddenly halting the growth of their children. Fear of these constantly hovered over their lives, and many precautions were taken against them.

At one of the festivals occurring in the early part of the native year, certain ceremonies were enacted with the aim of promoting the growth of their food, plants, and also their children. At the break of day, people would go out into the fields and tug lightly at some of the newly developed plants, or pull them out with their roots, and offer them in clusters in various temples.

At the end of this particular ceremony, after the children had taken their portion of food at the dining table, the parents might tug at or stretch their limbs and each part of their extremities separately. Thus the growth of the child was to coincide with that of the young maize. Then they raised each part of the body from the ground several times and finally lifted the child high, with hands over each of the child's ears. the fulfilling of this ceremony named Teizcalanaliztli, was supposed to warrant the growth of the children for the new year.

This very same rite was performed during or after an earthquake, to prevent a sudden halt in the child's growth. Another of their superstitions pertaining to growth, Tecuencholhuiliztli, taught that if anyone stepped over a child who was lying down or sitting, its ability to grow would be halted, and the child would be small for the remainder of its life. The remedy however was to step back over the child in the opposite direction.

When a child was ill, a superstitious rite was performed four times to insure the cure, in which strings of soft cotton were tied around its neck, wrists, and ankles. To the cotton was hung also a small ball of copal, or incense. These were worn by the child for the number of days under a favorable sign fixed by a priest-astrologer, and then removed by the latter and burned in the capulco, a small neighboring temple.

On four special days every year, the souls of the women who had died in childbirth were thought to come down to earth and inflict dangerous diseases, commonly paralysis, upon any child who happened to pass before them. On these days, parents kept their children out of harm's way by keeping them indoors, and appeased these malignant "goddesses" by adorning their places of prayer with flowers.

There was also the custom of sticking a number of feathers on the shoulders, arms and legs, of the children during one of their ceremonial rites for the purpose of preserving their children from these evils.

During the feast of Nei Tocoztli, all women who had begotten children during the preceding year purified themselves by walking in solemn parade after twilight, amid blazing torches, and placed sacrificial gifts in all oratories of the temples of the four quarters of the city.

The Aztecs regarded dreams as divine revelations, and if a dream involved the loss of teeth, it was looked upon as a sign of imminent death in the family. A dream of eating meat implied the death one's husband or wife. A dream of being swept away by water meant loss of property. A dream of flying in the air made one apprehensive for the safety of one's life.

As additional evidence of how the Aztecs regarded dreams as divine revelation, and the importance they attached to them, we find the story of how Montezuma, disturbed by mysterious omens, summoned all the old men, women and magicians, to give an account of what they might dream, or had dreamt within the duration of the prior month.

In view of the predominant belief that dreams contained important and grave forewarnings from a divine source, the demand to make known such dreams, for the use of the tribe, to the war-chief, was natural.

Certain men were especially adept in the explanation and interpretation of dreams to such an extent that they were frequently called upon for such purposes. If these interpreters declined to yield to such petitions, it was within the power of the ruler to deal with them as persons guilty of treason, and confine them, or worse, to avert harm to the tribe and its leaders.

As noted in the preceding chapter, when twins were born, one was usually killed. The surviving twin was forced to face many hardships throughout life and had to undergo a peculiar sort of training because of the many superstitions surrounding his birth.

His physical presence was expected to bring about a number of unusual and powerful influences. For example, if he drew near a steam bath or temazcalli, while it was being made hot, its temperature was often perceived to have become lowered, in spite of the fact that it had been hot only minutes before.

This was especially true when a twin chanced to be one of the bathers. The twin was seen to be in a position to correct this condition by dipping his hands into water and moistening the inside of the steam bath, sprinkling it four times, after which its coldness was terminated, and it became fully as hot as before, perhaps even hotter.

If the twin came into a house where rabbit's wool, or tochimitl, was going through the process of being dyed, at once the dye process was thought to be ruined, and the material irreparably spotted, particularly if the color of the dye was red. It also was believed that if maize-cakes were being cooked at the time of a twin's entrance into a home, an evil spell would be cast upon all who dwelled therein, and on the pot in which they were being cooked.

Happily for the twin, he was able to rise to the situation in both cases, and was in a position to amend the supposed evils brought about by his existence. In the latter case, all that was necessary was the rekindling of the fire under the pot. If the maize-cakes or tamales happened to have been placed in the pot in his presence, it became necessary for him to throw one of them into the fire, otherwise not a single one of them could be presumed safe for eating.

If we are to gather from the above that twins were not desirable guests, still less desirable were the dreaded visits of those perceived to be immoral persons, scornfully named "tlacolli." If such a person came into the court of a dwelling where little chickens were just in the act of emerging from their shells, these signs were seen as indications of the infidelity of either the husband or wife.

The ancient Aztecs were firmly convinced of the truth of the saying, "Coming events cast their shadows beforehand," believing in many omens by which the future could be predicted. The cries of wild animals or strange humming noises heard after dark were looked upon as evil signs forewarning of bad fortune, disaster, death or slavery, to some unfortunate member of the family.

The harsh shrill cries of an owl heard after nightfall was looked upon with similar foreboding. A small owl was considered to be a herald of the "Lord of the land of the dead," and it was assumed that he passed his time flying back and forth between the two worlds. His screams, and the scratching of his claws upon the rooftop proclaimed the coming of death.

The Mexicans, however, had conceived two sentences containing words of sharp reproach directed at the owlet, one symbolic expression for the man's use, another for women, and by declaring these aloud, it was believed possible to ward off the imminent catastrophe.

The dream specter of a female dwarf was also taken as a sign of impending doom. This ghost-like apparition, was often represented as having long hair coming down to its waist, walking with short steps, closer and closer to the person sleeping. It always succeeded in eluding capture, and disappeared and reappeared suddenly.

The entrance of a strange insect named Pinaviztli into a house was greeted as a bad sign by the inhabitants. Resembling a spider, but being the size of a mouse, with a hairless, partly red and black body, the Pinaviztli was able to exert negative influences which could be overcome only by specific acts. A cross leading to the four cardinal points of the world was marked on the floor, and the insect placed in its center. The man of the house, after first spitting on it, would put to it the following question: "Why hast thou come?"

The next step was to observe in what direction the insect would go. If it moved to the north, it was seen as a sign that the man was fated to die sooner rather than later. If it moved in another direction, it was recognized as a sign that he would meet with some other mishap of lesser importance.

Other natives dealt with it by pouncing upon it, passing a hair through its body, fastening it to a stick, and allowing it to hang until the following day. If the insect succeeded in disappearing, it was believed that some harm would befall the family. If it was still there, however, they were encouraged, and after throwing some wine on it to intoxicate it, were certain that the omen was harmless.

The discovery of an ant nest in a dwelling was regarded as a sign that some jealous or spiteful person had placed it there with the wicked intention of causing trouble to come to the household. Similarly, the presence of a frog or a mouse was attributed to the same cause, and in these instances the natives generally consulted the diviners immediately, to procure charms that would neutralize the evil omen.

The presence of rats was dreaded by the ancient Mexicans, for they were of the firm opinion that the rats had the special endowment of knowing whenever a member of a household had committed adultery. In such supposed situations, they very quickly appeared on the scene, gnawing holes in the petticoat of the wife if unfaithful, or in the cloak of the husband if he were the guilty one.

It can easily be surmised that this superstition must have been the cause of many baseless matrimonial recriminations. It was also believed that anyone, having partaken of a piece of food that had been gnawed by a rat, would be erroneously charged with theft, or some other felony—a rather serious matter, in view of the fact that the punishment inflicted for theft was death.

Before the setting of traps for the purpose of ridding the home of rats, the ancient Aztecs would first put the corn-grinding stone roller outside the house, or else it was believed the roller would forewarn the rats of the peril in store for them.

Marital infidelity, it was believed, could also be detected by the deformation of the wool which would come to view without fail in any piece of goods being woven for either the husband or wife. (It would not be amiss at this point to mention that adultery was punishable by death.

Parings of one's nails were thrown into the lake as a gift to the Ahuitzol, a water monster who appears frequently in Mexican folklore, for it was only after receiving this gift which formed the chief food of this monster, that the latter would permit the donor's nails to grow satisfactorily.

No person was permitted to wear sandals when he approached a hen that was hatching, for it was believed that if he did so, no chickens would be forthcoming from the eggs. If by any chance some were hatched, it was believed they would die quickly. By placing an old pair of sandals close to the hen house, however, the situation could be remedied.

Young maidens, upon being introduced into the workings of the kitchen and other domestic duties, were informed that it was essential to breathe in a strong manner upon maize which was just about to be placed into the pot to be boiled, because this would give it courage and take away its fear of being cooked.

Another one of the many superstitions prevailing among the Aztecs was one similar to the breaking of a mirror, and that was that the grinding-stone portended the death of the owner or someone of the household.

In addition, another popular belief held that persons eating green corn at night would suffer from toothache. It was usual therefore, to heat the ears of corn before eating after twilight, an undoubtedly wise choice quite apart from superstitious reasons.

When a person chanced to sneeze, it was regarded as a sign that someone was expressing some evil about him, or that he was being talked about by one or more persons.

During hailstorms, it was the custom of owners of maize or bean fields to set about protecting their crops from complete ruin by strewing ashes in the courtyard of their houses. During earthquakes, the natives forestalled the "carrying away" of their valued belongings by taking water into their mouths, blowing out and scattering drops of water over the thresholds and lintels of their houses.

It is difficult to ascertain from the early records how much of this kind of knowledge was taught consciously by the parents to the youngsters at this period of their lives. Very likely, much was learned by example and casual observation of elders, and by unconscious absorption.

During such situations, children are usually unaware that they are passing through any type of learning process and picking up various bits of knowledge. Very frequently, not only does the child have no notion of this fact, but the "instructor" is in an equal degree unaware that he or she is imparting anything. This "unconscious" form of education plays a large part in the lives of all peoples.

4

Social and Moral Education

The ancient Aztecs placed great emphasis on instruction in morals and manners, and this training constituted a most important part of their education. Parents endeavored to teach their children good habits of polite speech, and resorted to severe punishments for any breach of good conduct.

Children caught in a lie were exposed to asphyxiating smoke, symbolizing their obfuscation of the truth. They were taught to be quiet, modest, reserved in the presence of parents and grownups, and as a result in their early years, scarcely dared to speak out.

Respect and esteem for their parents were bred within them, and they were to guide their actions so as never to bring dishonor upon their family. Unquestionable obedience to parents was looked upon as one of the cardinal virtues of childhood; quarreling and squabbling were discouraged at all times by punishment.

Extreme abuse of, disrespect to, or the raising of hands to parents could result in death or disinheritance. As a matter of fact, if the children of the lower castes during their early years proved incorrigible, the parents were permitted to place them into slavery.

In the upper classes, children could be punished by beatings. It was not uncommon for the more mature youths who proved unmanageable to their parents to be strangled, or sent to the frontiers, or placed on the front of battles, that they might be killed.

Their hygienic moral precepts included good manners at the dining table, cleanliness with frequent bathing, and the prohibition of drinking wine to all except the elders, save for certain festival days.

There is ample evidence demonstrating that Aztec parents harbored the most tender affection and love for their children in spite of their harshness in matters of discipline. They were said to have spoken to the children with great warmth, and frequently used such endearing expressions as "gold bead"—teocuitla cuzcetl, or "jewel"—chalchihuitl, or quetzalli—which, used in a figurative sense, signified "precious beloved child, beloved daughter, beloved son, dear little dove."

When children attained a mature age, they were given instructions and advice through exhortation—many of which, loosely translated, follow. These exhortations were understanding, wise, sensible, and admirable, and, softened by affectionate expressions, revealed the complete measure of a parent's love. They were given at a time, chosen by the parent, when their children began to exhibit (and exercise) reason.

The following counsels, or so-called exhortations of the parents to the children were obtained from the Aztecs themselves by the very first Catholic friars who were occupied in converting them to Christianity, particularly Motolinia, Olmos, and Sahagun. They had mastered the Aztec language, and sought most industriously to acquire a similar knowledge of their manners and customs.

The underlying purpose of these early Spanish missionaries, in gathering this information, was to pass it on to their fellow-workers, to enable them to perceive any remaining signs of pagan and superstitious beliefs that persisted among the natives, so that these latter could be dealt with effectively.

Here now, some of these exhortations, liberally translated:

"My son," said the Aztec father, "who are come into the light from the womb of thy mother like the chicken from the egg, and like it are preparing to fly through the world, we know not how long heaven will grant to us the enjoyment of that precious gem which we possess in thee; but, however short the period, we pray you will endeavor to live exactly, praying God continually to assist you. He created thee; thou art his property. He is thy Father, and loves thee still more than I do; repose in Him thy thoughts, and day and night direct thy sighs to Him. Reverence and salute thy elders, and hold no one in contempt. To the poor and distressed be not dumb, but rather use words of comfort. Honor all persons, particularly thy parents, to whom thou owe obedience, respect and service.

"Guard against imitating the example of those wicked sons, who, like brutes that are deprived of reason, neither reverence their parents, listen to their instructions, nor submit to their correction; because, whoever follows their steps will have an unhappy end, will die in desperate manner, or will be killed and devoured by wild beasts."

(It is the author's belief that quite often a formal moral instruction will inevitably bore a young recipient into rebellion, thus defeating its end; an age-old conundrum. Of course this has never prevented one's elders from pouring forth interminable streams of pedantic counsel for the orientation of the younger generations. The more prolix the advice, the most likely to do the least good.)

The exhortations continue:

"Mock not, my son, the aged or imperfect. Scorn him not who you see fall into some folly or transgression, nor make him reproaches, but restrain thyself, and beware lest thou fall into the same error which offends thee in another. Go not where thou are not called, nor interfere in that which does not concern thee. Endeavor to manifest thy good breeding in all thy words and actions. I

"In conversation, do not lay thy hands upon another; nor speak too much, nor interrupt or disturb another's discourse. if thou hear anyone talking foolishly, and it is not thy business to correct him, keep silence; but if it does concern thee, consider first what thou are to say, and do not speak arrogantly that thy correction may be well received.

"When anyone discourses with thee, bear him attentively, and hold thyself in an easy attitude, neither playing with thy feet, putting thy mantle to thy mouth, nor spitting too often, nor looking about you here and there, nor rising up frequently if thou art sitting; for such actions are indications of levity and low breeding.

"When thou art at table do not eat voraciously, nor show thy displeasure if anything displeases thee. If anyone comes unexpectedly to dinner with thee, share with him what thou hast, and when any person is entertained by thee, do not fix thy looks upon him.

"In walking, look where thou go, that thou may not push against anyone. If thou see another coming thy way, go a little aside to give him room to pass. Never step before the elders, unless it be necessary, or that they order you to do so. When thou sit at a table with them, do not eat or drink before them, but attend to them in a becoming manner, that thou may merit their favor.

"When they give thee anything, accept it with tokens of gratitude; if the present is great, do not become vain or fond of it. If the gift is small, do not despise it nor be troubled nor occasion displeasure to them who favor thee. If thou becomes rich, do not grow indolent, nor scorn the poor; for those very gods who deny riches to others in order to give to thee, offended by thy pride will take them from thee again to give to others.

"Support thyself by thy own labors, for then thy food will be sweeter. I, my son, have supported thee hitherto with my sweat, and have omitted no duty of a father; I have provided thee with everything necessary without taking it from others. Do so likewise.

"Never tell a falsehood; because a lie is a heinous sin. When it is necessary to communicate to another what has been imparted to thee, tell the simple truth without any addition. Speak ill of no one. Do not take notice of the failings which thou observe in others, if thou art not called upon to correct them.

"Be not a news carrier, nor a sower of discord. When thou bear any embassy, and to whom it is borne is enraged, and speaks contemptuously of those who sent thee, do not report such an answer, but endeavor to soften him and dissemble as much as possible that which thou bear, that thou may not raise discord and speed calumny of which thou may afterwards repent.

"Stay no longer than is necessary in the marketplace; for in such places there is the greatest danger of contracting vices.

"When thou art offered an employment, imagine that the proposal is made to try thee; then accept it not hastily, although thou know thyself more fit than others to exercise it, but excuse thyself until thou are obliged to accept it; thus thou wilt be more esteemed.

"Be not dissolute; because thou wilt thereby incense the gods, and they will cover thee with infamy. Refrain thyself, my son, as thou are yet young, and wait until the girl, whom the gods destined for thy wife, arrives at a suitable age; leave that to their care, as they know how to order everything properly. When the time for thy marriage is come, dare not to make it without the consent of thy parents, otherwise, it will have an unhappy issue.

"Steal not, nor give thyself up to gaming; otherwise thou wilt be a disgrace to thy parents, whom thou ought rather to honor for the education they have given thee. If thou wilt be virtuous, thy example will put the wicked to shame.

"No more, my son; enough has been said in discharge of the duties of a father. With these counsels I wish to fortify thy mind. Refuse them not, nor act in contradiction to them; for on them thy life, and all thy happiness depend!"

And some of the exhortations from an Aztec mother to her daughter, again liberally translated:

"My daughter," said the mother, "born of my substance, brought forth with my pains, and nourished with my milk, I have endeavored to bring thee up with the greatest possible care, and thy father has wrought and polished thee like an emerald, that thou may appear in the eyes of men a jewel of virtue.

"Strive always to be good; for otherwise who will have thee for a wife? Thou will be rejected by everyone. Life is a thorny laborious path, and it is necessary to exert all our powers to obtain the goods which the gods are willing to yield to us; we must not therefore be lazy or negligent but diligent in everything.

"Be orderly and take pains to manage the economy of the house. Give water to thy husband for his hands, and make bread for thy family. Wherever you go, go with modesty and composure, without hurrying thy steps, or laughing with those whom thou meet, neither fixing thy looks upon them, nor casting thy eyes thoughtlessly, first to one side and then to another, that thy reputation may not be sullied; but give a courteous answer to those who salute and put any question to you.

"Employ yourself diligently in spinning and weaving, in sewing and embroidering; for by these arts you will gain esteem, and all the necessities of food and clothing. Do not give yourself too much to sleep, nor seek the shade, but go in the open air and there repose thyself.

"In whatever you do, encourage not evil thoughts; but attend solely to the service of the gods and the giving of comfort to your parents. If thy mother or father calls, do not stay to be called twice, but go quickly to know their pleasure, that you may not disoblige them by slowness. Return no insolent answers nor show any want of compliance; but if you cannot do what they command, make a modest excuse.

"If another is called and does not come quickly, hear what is ordered, go quickly, and do it yourself. Never offer yourself to do that which you cannot do. Deceive no one, for the gods see all your actions. Live in peace with everyone, and love everyone sincerely and honestly that you may be loved by them in return.

"Be not greedy of the goods you have. If you see anything presented to another, give way to no mean suspicions; for the gods to whom every good belongs, distribute everything as they please. If you would avoid the displeasure of others, let none meet with it from thee.

"Guard against improper familiarities with men; nor yield to the guilty wishes of thy heart, or thou wilt be the reproach of thy family, and will pollute thy mind as mud does water. Keep not company with dissolute, lying or idle women; otherwise they will infallibly infect thee by their example. Attend upon thy family, and do not go on slight occasions out of thy house, nor be seen wandering through the streets, or in the marketplace; for in such places you will meet thy ruin.

"Remember that vice, like the poisonous herb, brings death to those who take it; and when it once harbors in the mind, it is difficult to expel it. If in passing through the street you meet with a forward youth who appears agreeable to the eye, give him no correspondence, but dissemble, and pass on. If he says anything to you, take no heed of him nor his words; and if he follows you, turn not your face to look at him, lest that might inflame his passion the more. If you behave so, he will soon turn and let you proceed in peace.

"Enter not, without some urgent motive, into another's house, that nothing may be either said or thought injurious to your honor; but if you enter into the house of your relations, salute them with respect and do not remain idle, but immediately take up a spindle or do any other thing that is useful.

"When you are married, respect your husband, obey him, and diligently do what he commands. Avoid incurring his displeasure, nor show thyself passionate or ill-natured; but receive him fondly to thy arms, even if he is poor and lives at thy expense. If thy husband occasions in thee any disgust, let him not know thy displeasure when he commands thee to do anything, but dissemble it at that time, and afterwards tell him with gentleness what vexed thee, that he may be won by thy mildness, and offend thee no further.

"Dishonor him not before others; for thou also would be dishonored. If anyone comes to visit thy husband, accept the visit kindly and show all the civility you can. If thy husband is foolish, be thou discreet. If he fails in the management of wealth, admonish him of his failings; but if he is totally incapable of taking care of his estate, take that charge upon thyself, attending carefully to his possessions, and never omit to pay the workmen punctually. Take care not to lose anything through negligence.

"Embrace, my daughter, the counsels I have given thee; I am already advanced in life, and have had sufficient dealings with the world. I am thy mother, and wish that thou may live well. Fix my precepts well in thy heart, for then thou wilt live happily. If, by not listening to me, or by neglecting my instructions any misfortunes befall thee, the fault will be thine, and the evil also. Enough, my child. May the gods prosper thee."

To place these exhortations in further context, it would be quite easy to suspect that some of the preceding prayers were the invention—not of pre-Conquest Aztecs, but of Christians. If we had not Sahagun's explicit statements of the great care which he exercised in securing his information from the Aztecs, and checking it with other authorities, this would seem very likely.

It is difficult, however, to see why he should be inclined to paint an unduly favorable picture of the paganism of the Mexicans, which the early priests appeared to abominate, by putting worthy Christian prayers into the mouths of priests and priestesses.

These moral virtues stressed by the Aztec parents in their exhortations to the children are, of course, immediately recognizable as the same ones honored throughout Christendom today, almost without exception. Reverence and fear of the deities; love and respect for parents; consideration for one's elders; pity for the poor and helpless; the fulfillment and payment of one's debts; horror of vice; constant employment to flee idleness; to speak the truth always; to proceed in every-thing with moderation, subjecting one's actions to reason and justice; to mind one's own business; to show good breeding in all words and actions; to be chaste, truthful, hospitable, compassionate, temperate, prudent, charitable, industrious, thrifty, patient, meek, loyal, dutiful, patriotic, tactful, not be greedy, deceitful, obstinate, dissolute, vacillating, bear falsehoods, nor to gossip.

Many of the qualities and characteristics set up by the Aztecs as standards, undoubtedly were influenced by the demands of their religious, social, political and industrial occurrences of everyday life.

For example, since they were living in a state of almost continuous military preparedness and activity, the virtues which the Aztecs esteemed most were an attitude of reverence for the tribal war-god, courage, a willingness to die on the battlefield or the sacrificial altar, loyalty to the group, absolute unquestioning obedience to those in authority and to the laws of the tribe and army, merciless-ness towards foes, and consideration for comrades.

We can also understand easily why in their handicrafts and industrial occupa-tions, skilled craftsmanship was admired and respected, while theft, slovenly work, and work were considered heinous.

The methods used to elect the tribal chief or "king" specifically included those qualities above, which the ancient Mexicans respected most, and looked for in making their selection. In order to elect another chief, the most influential leaders of the town came together in the royal houses to deliberate, and select the most noble of the lineages of deceased lords; the most valiant, skilled in warfare, dar-ing, spirited, not in the habit of over-indulging in wine-drinking; the most pru-dent, learned, well-spoken; the one who would take into account the condition of the orphans, the widows, the old men and women who could no longer work. In other words, the candidates who most represented the ideal values they respected most.

Of course, all that being said, there was the matter of human sacrifice.

Today, even as in past centuries, the Aztec civilization is severely condemned by historians for its religious act of human sacrifice. Those who have deprecated the culture of the ancient Mexicans have taken this custom as the basis for their judgment, stressing the cruelty of human sacrifice on the one hand while neglect-ing to give full weight to the achievements and progress these remarkable people had attained before the arrival of the Conquistadors to America.

Exactly at what time the Mexican races began to offer human sacrifices we do not know. The Aztecs came into the Valley of Mexico as the last of the invading Nahuans. Weak in strength, they were given no alternative other than to settle on poor land in the lake areas. Some time later, they triumphed in a small encounter with a neighboring tribe, and sacrificed some of the prisoners. From then on, their rise to political domination started, and the association of human sacrifice with good fortune thereafter became manifest to them.

As their numbers increased, their need for additional land and food increased proportionately, and they found it necessary to conquer in order to maintain their economic well-being. Concurrently, they believed that an unstinting human sacrifice was necessary for the holding of the goodwill of their gods.

Obviously, the act of sacrificing a human life is always cruel and obscene; but the Aztec sacrificial rites were not merely the promptings of a vain and blood-thirsty cruelty. They were motivated by a religious belief so strong it impelled them to commit every kind of excess in order to propitiate their gods and ensure good crops.

The Aztecs also believed that if certain parts of their enemies' bodies, the legs, thighs and arms, were eaten, they would acquire the strength that their victims formerly possessed.

A brief survey of the juridical system of the ancient Mexicans might be in order at this juncture, since law is the expression of social conscience. Few if any actual written laws, or "penal codes" are said to have survived. Instead, numerous paintings which represented their manners and customs, as well as scenes of everyday life, provide many details concerning their legal institutions, including the forms of declaring war, methods of holding prisoners and hostages, the inter-tribal recognition of certain privileges for merchants, and diplomatic relations among the different tribes.

The paintings suggest that minor cases involving members of the same ward were adjudged by a gathering of the clan elders or by a popularly elected magistrate called "tecuhtli." Next in importance were the district courts located in each of the four major quarters of Tenochtitlan, and in each of the important regional areas outside of the capital.

Their sessions were held every day. Each of these courts was presided over by a chief magistrate, and two assisting judges. Each judge had his own bailiff and deputies who were entrusted with the work of summoning necessary parties, arresting delinquents, and following through on all judgments. The courts were closed on special occasions, such as public sacrifices and festival days when the presence of the magistrates was required.

The judges were selected from the ranks of the sons of the well-to-do, and nobles who had received their education in the Calmecac, usually on the recommendation of the Mexicatlotencatzin, chief administrator of the temple school.

In addition, the other qualifications for this type of civil service job included proven characters of trustworthiness, honesty, sincerity, and sobriety.

Young men who were intended for the magistry were led to the courts to hear the laws of the tribe being interpreted, and to study the practice and forms of judicature.

In the sixtieth painting of the Mendoza Codex, there is depicted four magistrates considering a case, and directly in back of them there are four young men observing the process and judgment. The judges were distinguished by a badge of a certain ornamental mantle. They received sufficient support from the produce of certain lands set aside for that purpose, so that there would be no temptation to accept bribes.

They were not to receive gifts, and were severely punished if it was discovered that they had committed an injustice, or had otherwise obstructed justice in any of the matters which came under their jurisdiction.

A single court of appeal ranking over these district courts, and also consisting of a chief magistrate and two assisting judges, was to be found in the chief ruler's palace. This special court considered appeals from the decisions of the district courts, and tried these cases, apparently in secret sessions, in which members of the nobility were brought up on charges. Immediately upon the rendering of a verdict in the case of appeal, sentence was carried out.

The highest court of authority described, was that presided over by the snake-woman (Cihuacoatl), the Aztec co-ruler, with the assistance of thirteen elders. One of its most important functions seems to have been the trying of the appeals of the nobility from the decision of the appeals court, which for the nobility was the original court of hearing.

The procedure followed in the courts was to have all parties concerned present orally their complaints and defenses. Proofs were asked for and submitted. Testimony under oath served as evidence. Verdicts were usually rendered immediately.

Early historians have said that the cases were depicted on paper, and the case thus put on record for transmittal to a higher court, but Aztec hieroglyphic writing was so unwieldy that it is hard to conceive of much detail being noted in such records. However, by the combined system of picture writing and glyphs, it would be possible to record the prisoner's name, his crime, as for instance the theft of property, the town where the crime was committed, the name of the victim, and the sentence if it were a case of some fine or death.

No records of this nature have survived, but there is no reason to doubt that if they ever existed, they were used as aids for memory.

The common laws of the Aztecs were perpetuated in their minds not only by traditional stories, but also through constant oral transmission from the heads of families to the children for the quite obvious reason of preventing them from violating any of the laws. Justice was applied with extreme strictness. All of the major crimes committed against society were made punishable by death. Prisons as we know them were practically unknown.

The nearest thing to them were dark wooden cages which served as places of temporary confinement, and had entrances that have been compared to pigeon holes.

These "prisons" are described as places of temporary confinement because the prisoners were kept there not for punishment but pending immediate execution or sacrifice.

Any prisoner left there for any length of time invariably died of hunger, filth, or infection. Permanent confinement simply meant death.

Civil and penal laws were concerned with many matters ranging from domestic relations, family problems, marriage, individual property, communal property, contracts, inheritances, propriety of morals, to the more severe cases of theft, adultery and murder. Stealing was punishable by slavery or death, in accordance with the extent of the crime. The Aztecs could not have feared theft very much since their houses had no doors.

They merely placed two sticks in the entrance, and these seemed to serve as sufficient protection as a taboo. Robbery in temples and in the markets was summarily punished by death. Theft of gold was punished by sacrifice to Xipe, the patron god of the goldsmiths. The theft of a large quantity of corn, such as twenty ears or more, or the spiteful uprooting of crops in the fields also resulted in a sentence of death.

Capital crimes also included the misuse of official dress or ornaments, the removal of boundaries from another's land, the tampering with established measures, the improper care of a ward's property on the part of a guardian, and the practice of witchcraft.

This respect for all property-holdings, and the severity of these last laws can be traced back to their early days of difficulty and starvation, when the Aztecs first arrived in the valley of Mexico.

Harsh penalties were exacted for excessive indulgence in intoxicating liquors: death by garroting for youths; loss of rank and seizure of property for the older men and persons of importance. Only the very old, past seventy, were permitted to drink without fear of consequence, perhaps because it was thought they were near death anyway.

This prohibition was absolute. If anyone drank pulque without having the necessary permission, there was no appeal possible. They were killed in sight of all. In order to scare the people thoroughly, their judges took them with their hands tied, to the marketplace, and there warned the people, saying that no one except the old men and women should drink pulqe. After this, their executioners, called Quauhnochtli, broke their necks, or otherwise dispatched them.

An explanation for the severe civil punishments inflicted upon transgressors of their code concerning drunkenness, lay in the outcomes the ancient Mexicans attributed to intoxication. They believed that it led to many accidents, drownings, transgressions of law, deeds of violence, theft, highway robbery, adultery, rape and suicide.

Social pressure against excess drinking was exerted openly even by the tribal chieftain, when in an inaugural address, he admonished the youths of the nation, the warriors, and especially the "nobles" not to make fools of themselves through drinking and fleshly vices.

In spite of all the strict restrictions against pulque, the manufacture and sale of it was a thriving industry, and a profit-making occupation in ancient Mexico. Our earliest sources mention that in certain markets, large stone vessels containing wine for public sale could often be found, though probably not in full view.

Concerning the actions of gamblers, wastrels and other misfits, the Aztecs hung or otherwise severely punished those sons who had squandered the property left by their fathers, or destroyed the arms, jewels, or other remarkable things that their fathers had bequeathed them.

Murder was invariably punished by death, even if the murderer was a noble, and his victim but a slave. Adulterers were stoned to death after proof had come forth from independent witnesses, or after confession from either of the guilty persons. While members of the nobility could not escape the punishment if condemned, they were not killed publicly but were accorded the privilege of being executed in private, usually by strangulation.

The injured husband who attempted to take the law into his own hands and kill his wife or her lover, was punished with death, even if he had come upon them in the act. It would seem that the tribe considered the crime as one against itself, more so than against the husband.

While monogamy was the general practice among the ancient Aztecs, the well-to-do and the nobles often had several wives. Divorce was not uncommon, but as a general rule was not encouraged by the magistrates and the community.

In addition to the courts enumerated above, there were various tribunals that had jurisdiction over special cases; the councils of twelve old men who handled disputes in each clan market; military courts which dealt with military matters of crime, such as trying warriors for cowardice, treachery, conspiracy and sedition, the penalty for which was death. The merchants as a privileged caste in the Aztec social organization, also had their own judges who settled independently all difficulties that arose between members of the guild.

One of the most notable parts however of Aztec law was that concerning the institution of slavery. The ancient Mexicans recognized several kinds of slaves: prisoners of war who were nearly always destined for sacrifice; persons who had lost their freedom by conviction for some crime; poverty-stricken persons who had deliberately given up their freedom; and children sold by their own parents, for various reasons such as incorrigibility and destitution.

Often, after destructive droughts or disastrous floods which deprived the inhabitants of the valley their annual crops, fathers exchanged their services and those of their children in return for food, with members of other tribes more fortunate in possessing sufficient stores.

In this last instance, it was not an uncommon practice for the parents to send a younger brother as a substitute after having secured the consent of the master. In this manner, for periods of several years of service, the different children in the family could equalize the burden.

The institution of slavery among the Aztecs differed considerably from that prevailing in Europe and other parts of the world at that time, and the same conclusion holds today for our conception of slavery. The readiness on the part of a free man to assume the obvious disadvantages of servitude is made understandable by the mild form in which it prevailed.

There was no social stigma attached to being a slave. The Mexican term for slave was literally a "purchased man" or tlacotli. The agreement of sale or contract had to be carried out before as many as four authorized witnesses. The services to be performed and conditions under which he was to work were described with great exactitude For instance, in some cases, he could insist on no resale without his consent.

The slave was permitted to keep his own family, maintain his own home, possess property, and even granted the right to have other slaves. Furthermore, the children of slaves were born free.

Incorrigible slaves, such as those who broke their contracts repeatedly, could be "collared," that is be made to have their necks enclosed in a wooden yoke, which could then be fastened to a wall at night. Continued misbehavior on the part of the slave could result in his sale for sacrificial purposes, although such punishment was not general. Any "collared' slave who succeeded in escaping, and reached the palace of a tribal ruler without being intercepted by his master or his minions could be set completely free.

The flight of the slave, however, could not be obstructed by anyone else, not even the palace guards whom he passed, under liability of being enslaved in turn for such action. Slaves were seldom sold, unless hard times forced the master to that extreme.

Slaves were frequently granted freedom upon the death of their master, although if that was not done, they passed on to the heirs of the deceased. Occasionally, marriages were effected between owner and slave, or between the widow of a master and a slave she had inherited upon the death of her husband, since there existed no innate aversion based on differences of blood and race, nor stigma attached to slavery itself.

5

Religion in Aztec Life

It has been observed that primitive man, in his own setting, was very much occupied throughout his life with the satisfying of his daily wants, and with attempts to appease the "hostile influences" which surrounded him. There was no let-up in his constant watch regarding the latter, and it followed that his religious observances, therefore, consumed a considerable part of his day. His daily and seasonal activities like planting and reaping a harvest were always supplemented by prayer and offerings to the gods.

Since the ancient Aztecs were far more advanced in the scale of civilization than primitives while still retaining many of their characteristics, they had a religion that was correspondingly more complex. The Aztec religion was an aggregate of dissimilar elements.

Although we know that in later times the Aztecs possessed a highly organized militaristic state with an accompanying military theology, still basically, theirs was a typical agrarian society, with complicated ceremonies of imitative magic intended to create rain and to help the growth of crops.

It also included, however, many characteristics of primitive shamanism, and nature worship. Into this composite were merged many idolatrous elements, such as the reverence and worship of obsidian, or animals like the jaguar, humming bird, serpent, and of heavenly bodies, especially the sun, moon, nature spirits and true gods.

Gradually, the clan leaders had combined the different simple components into a system, had devised an impressive speculative theology, with certain gods more important than others, and had arrayed the barbaric rites with significant and mystical learning, all of which appealed directly to the understanding of the masses. This transformed elaborate ritual continued to be under the guidance of the clan leaders who became part of an organized priesthood.

Governmental and religious functions became inextricably interwoven, since the same individuals, the chief men of the clans performed both sets of duties. A true theocracy rule by the gods with the priest-chiefs as intermediaries, became the outcome of such a social arrangement, and the tribal policies came to be dictated almost as much by religious as by political considerations.

The "sovereign" deemed himself honored if granted the privilege of assisting in the services of the temple. Instead of restricting the authority of the priests, the tribal ruler, if not of an extraordinarily dominating personality would often yield in his views to theirs. The priests soon came to constitute the learned and most powerful class. In their hands lay the education of the young, and the destiny of their society.

They tempered the men and women as they desired, instilling within them a deep respect for their gods and their ministers. They were the advisers of all classes, the most humble as well as the most distinguished, and by their seemingly blameless conduct, held the devotion of the people.

So strict were the priests in the practice of honesty and chastity, that any deviation there from could be punished with death. It was felt that if they were there as ministers of god, and they were beheld indulging in vicious habits and profane behaviors, it would ultimately lead their followers to undervalue their faith, and treat it with derision.

The priesthood organized and directed the celebration of public religious festivals around which most of their religious life revolved, and which were held in each of the eighteen months of the Mexican calendar. These festivals were either of a fixed nature, to be held on some particular day of the month, or movable, attached to some signs of their calendar, which did not match with the same days in every year.

The perpetual succession of these external ceremonies in which the people participated, linked religion with their most personal affairs, and thus, one of their strongest characteristics was their strong attachment to these ceremonies.

The ushering in of every new day by a national sacrifice to the sun, and the feeding of the idols, in addition to the eminent and conspicuous position of the tribal temples, also contributed towards keeping religion uppermost in the minds of the people.

From an educational viewpoint, the festivals alone were of significance because they probably helped stimulate and develop the tribal and individual religious consciousness more than any other factor. Parents were directed to instruct their children in advance or during the celebration in the origin and meaning of the festival. This home instruction was supplemented by lessons given in public by priests and scribes.

The number of images by which the Aztec deities were personified were numberless, and it seems that the most important duty of the priesthood, and the chief ceremony of the Aztec people, in addition to prayers, fasts, kneeling, prostrations, and other austere rites, was the offering of sacrifice to them.

These were made constantly for numerous reasons, chief of which were to procure favors from the deities, or to express gratitude for favors which had already been granted. The sacrifices differed in numbers, place, and kind. Human sacrifices, which loomed in their eyes as the most important, ceremonially, and which has drawn the most condemnation throughout the centuries after their discovery, differed according to the circumstances of the festival.

The method of the sacrifice, generally, in killing the victim, was to place his body upon a temple altar, cut open the breast to get at the heart, cut it, remove it, and offer it to the sun and idols.

Other methods of disposing of the victims doomed for sacrifice included drowning in the lake, imprisonment in caverns to be left to die of hunger, and the gladiatorial sacrifice, resembling fully the old Roman combats.

Children were frequently sacrificed during agricultural festivals for the purpose of hastening the rainy season. The Aztecs searched for a great many infants, buying them from their mothers and choosing especially those which had two twisted tufts of hair on their heads, and infants born under a lucky sign.

These were thought to be more agreeable sacrifices to the gods, to make them grant water at the most opportune times. They carried these infants up to the high mountains to kill them, choosing those areas the priests had designated for the purpose. There on those mountain tops, the priests tore out the hearts of the infants, lifted them toward the heavens and importuned their gods to favor them.

It seems that the mountains were selected for these particular sacrifices because they were regarded as active agents in the production of rain, attracting and gathering the clouds, as they did, around their peaks. The ancient Mexicans looked upon these parts of the mountains with reverence because it was around them that the sky and heavens met, and yielded the showers which endowed the earth with new life.

While pilgrimages and sacrifices to the mountain tops were accepted as a part of the duties of the Aztec priesthood, in the cities it was it was the pyramid temple which answered the purpose as a suitable substitute for the mountain. It was in the temples that a large, if not the major portion of all their sacrifices usually took place, upon the altar set aside for the purpose.

The altar of the greater temple of Mexico was a stone convex in shape, green in color, three feet high, another three wide, and more than five feet long. The usual ministers of the sacrifice were six priests, chief of whom was the Topiltzin, whose dignity was preeminent and hereditary.

At every ceremony, the Topiltzin assumed the name of that god to whom the sacrifice was made.

For the performance of this function, he was clothed in a red habit, fringed with cotton, and on his head he wore a crown of green and yellow feathers. At his ears there hung golden earrings and green emeralds, and at his under-lip, a pendant of turquoise.

The other five ministers were dressed in white habits of the same make, but embroidered with black; their hair was wrapped up, their heads bound with leather thongs, their foreheads armed with little shields of paper painted various colors, and their bodies dyed black all over.

These ministers led the victims, often naked, to the upper area of the temple, and having pointed out to the bystanders the idol to whom the sacrifice was made, that they might pay their adoration to it, extended each victim upon the altar. Four priests held his legs and arms, and another kept his head firm with a wooden instrument made in the form of a coiled serpent placed around his neck. The body of the victim lay arched, the breast and belly being raised up and totally prevented from the least movement.

The Topiltzin then approached, and with a flint cutting knife, dexterously opened his breast and tore out his heart, which while yet palpitating, he offered to the sun. After the heart of the victim was elevated by the priest as an act of dedication towards the sun, thus gratifying and nourishing the sun with it, it was laid in the Quauhxicalli, the Mexican vessel for sacrificial blood. He followed this by burning it, preserving the ashes with the utmost veneration.

If the idol was gigantic and hollow, however, it was not unusual to introduce a portion of the victim's heart into its mouth, with a golden spoon. It was customary also, to anoint the lips of the idol, and the cornices of the sanctuary door with the victim's blood. If he was a prisoner of war, as soon as he was sacrificed, they cut off his head to preserve the skull, and threw the body down the stairs to the lower area, to be disposed of.

Sacrificial offerings were not restricted to humans. Quails and falcons were sacrificed to their war-lords; hares, rabbits, deer and coyote their god Mixcoatl. Every day at dawn, several priests greeted the sun's appearance with a sacrifice of quail. Then too, religious offerings were also made of flowers, plants, jewels, bread and prepared food.

Countless dishes and bowls of boiling food were found at the feet of the altars every morning, so that the rising steam might pass through the nostrils of the images and thus feed the eternal gods. Copal (incense) burning was the offering most practiced by the priests and commoners. The censers in all houses were used daily. The act was regarded as a sign of courtesy to the god, the nobility, and the officials of the tribe.

In a civilization which had reached a stage of development like that of the Aztecs, religion will be found manifesting itself in many different ways, usually in conformance with the different classes of the population.

The idols the Aztecs worshiped were numerous, and found in many places, especially in the temples of their demons, and in the courtyards, in the forests, large hills and ports, and in high mountains. Likewise, they had idols near the water, chiefly near mountains where they built their sacrificial altars.

At the crossroads in different sections of the towns, they had oratories in which there were idols of diverse forms and figures. Some had the shapes of bishops with mitres and croziers; others had figures of men. On these they threw wine, to celebrate the gods of wine. Some had the figures of women. Some had the shapes of wild beasts, lions, tigers, dogs, deer. Some had the shapes of serpents, and before these they placed strings of snake tails.

The early accounts of the constant succession of feasts and their attendant rites have given us the impression of a people solely occupied with the celebration of a prodigious and bloody worship.

Concerning the masses, and how they fit into this religious picture, we should probably not be far in error in supposing that the average layman managed to get around many of the taboos and omens of bad augury with as much success as the average citizen of the world today avoids strict application of the advanced idealism of whatever religion he or she subscribes to.

Whatever the priest and diviner thought, the man in the street probably reached the conclusion that the continuous round of feasts were made for man, and not man for them. It is easy to believe he compromised accordingly in their observance, devoutly participating in those which most closely affected their well-being, but inwardly little moved by the feasts of the warrior group.

His allegiances were many. Besides a multitude of lesser beings, nature spirits, guardian angels of households, clans and guilds, the ancient Mexicans paid homage to hundreds of true gods.

We find in the confusing multiplicity of these gods that their origins were several. Some can be traced as ancestors of certain races in their early history, and some personifications of natural forces, as the rain god. Others had an astronomical origin, and still others came into being from suggestive ceremonies like the worship of the maize plant as a "maize god."

Other deities dated from the dreams of priests, who then proclaimed their visions as divine revelation, painted a picture of it, and caused it to be adored. This instance throws an interesting light on the importance attached to visions by the priesthood, who resorted to fasting and certain vegetable drugs in order to induce them.

Still others may have been the outgrowth of the views of particular cults, and theological speculations. Through their early subjugation to neighboring tribes, and then later with their own rise, the subjecting in turn of other tribes, other deities were introduced from without. This process of uncertain fusion is mirrored by a marked disorder, and we find the different gods sometimes trodding on one another, with one god often emerging under various names and in several forms.

This occurs frequently because of their possessing several attributes, and in painting them in their codices, the one and the same god may be found several times under a different aspect, different color, and with the different names they were given for each characteristic.

We find that some divinities even enjoyed the same qualities with others. Confusion is also heightened by contradictions, for among their gods we find one who is supposed to have hated war and human sacrifice, and others who insisted upon human blood for sustenance, and promoted wars for the furtherance of their wishes. Among this aggregate of gods, no particular one was ever established as supreme in the eyes of all the people.

Four, however, towered over the rest.

Huitzilopochtli, or Humming-bird-on-the-Left, was the special tribal war god of the Aztecs, and in the eyes of the warrior nobility class, the supreme god. This "Mars of Mexico" was endowed with auxiliary solar, agrarian and hunting attributes.

It should be noted that the ancient Mexicans were wont to recognize two natures in their deities: a beneficent and a dread power, and it was the latter which predominated in their sentiments and conceptions. The maize plant, which gives food to all, occasions famine in the land, and the sun is the light swallowed up by the darkness. They conceived of no friendly character without at once seeing it converted into its opposite.

The Aztecs possessed no greater religious center than that of the main temple of the Huitzilopochtli cult, inasmuch as they had frequent occasion to petition their war god for their victories.

Tezcatlipoca, or Smoking Mirror, was the general, all-around powerful god of the Nahuan peoples, and was believed to be omnipotent, invisible, and ubiquitous; the Mexican Jupiter, "omniscient and all-seeing," he judged and punished sinners and humbled the proud, and ruled according to his pleasure.

He was also supposed to possess the power to grant to people wealth, military rank, distinction, and social position. His name was derived from the obsidian mirror which he carried, and in which it was thought he could see all that went on throughout the world. Forever young, he was supposed to personify the very breath of life, and also oversee the feasts and banquets, and patronize the military colleges.

In addition to being a sky-god, he must also have been connected with agriculture, because at festivals in his honor, his consorts dressed up as fertility goddesses, and he too, was known likewise, to be a god of drought and a rain-bringer.

It has been the subject of much debate whether or not at the time of the Spanish conquest, the Aztec religion was evolving toward monotheism, and that Tezcatlipoca was gradually on the road to becoming the one true god of the nobility.

Tlaloc, great god of water, rain, clouds, thunder and mountains, the "Mexican Neptune," with numerous lesser gods or tlalocs, was naturally of major importance to the agricultural classes, who were inhabitants of a somewhat dry region. It was he who also sent hail and lightning and storms on the waters, and all dangers of rivers and the sea.

Sharing with their war god Huitzilopochtli the great temple in the heart of the city, Tlaloc was the god of the common people as contrasted to the deities who were regarded favorably by the priests and nobility.

Quetzalcoatl, the "Plumed or feathered Serpent," special god of the priestly class, was to the mass of people, the god of wind and air, and sometimes a rain and thunder god. Worshiped over all of middle America, and associated with the Maya "Kukulcan," he is present in legend as perhaps the most extraordinary personage in ancient Mexican history; great emperor, priest, and culture hero of the Toltecs, artist and humanist philosopher.

From the early chroniclers we learn that the Indians pictured him as a tall large-bodied man, face hair, broad brow, large eyes, with long black hair and flowing beard.

The invention of the calendar was attributed to him, and so was the development of the different industrial arts, such as stone-cutting, engraving, the silversmith's craft, and the setting of precious stones.

He is also supposed to have taught the people agriculture, the art of government, and all priestly rites and sciences, and to have founded good and wise laws that helped promote trade and peace.

Known to be mild and gentle, he opposed sacrifices of living beings, human or animal, but offered to the gods instead, food, flowers, and incense. As a god, he was identified with the morning star, as well. By far, it is believed that the greatest of his attributes have to do with his character as a priest.

Quetzalcoatl was the priest-god eminent above all others.

Tlaloc and Quetzalcoatl are directly traceable in origin to an earlier period, and represent without question, the Toltec influence.

Huitzilopochtli and Tezcatlipoca typify the more militant actions of the Aztecs, after their number had grown to the stage where food had to be obtained by resorting to conquest or pillaging, and their worship promoted by a priesthood, which attempted to govern through the instilling of fear at home and violent dread abroad.

When the Aztecs had first entered the Valley of Mexico, they had brought with them a tribal god, Huitzilopochtli, who was looked upon by them as their personal leader, a god of hunting and war. After settling in the valley and adopting a settled form of life, they had turned to agriculture and the development of the arts and crafts, in the meanwhile accepting fully the worship of the two gods of the original inhabitants of the valley, Tlaloc and Quetzalcoatl, who exercised superintendence over war the respective occupations mentioned.

The Aztecs, in fact, displayed a notable tolerance and liberality in religious matters, and accepted more of the valley people's gods, and also, some of those of the tribes outside of the valley with whom they gradually came into contact.

Even if they did insist, however, upon the supremacy of their own tribal god Huitzilopochtli, still it is sufficiently meaningful that, when the great pyramid temple of Tenochtitlan was erected, the shrine of Tlaloc, the old agricultural rain-god of the Valley shared the conspicuous position at the highest part, with that of the tribal god of the Aztecs.

Of the two hundred plus divinities who made up the Mexican pantheon, some of the most prominent will be mentioned here.

The Ciuapipilti were all the women who died in childbirth, now glorified and declared goddesses. It was believed that they always traveled together through the air, and they possessed the power to be visible to those on earth whenever they so desired, and could cause boys and girls to be stricken, diseased, or to suffer from paralysis.

On those days when they were supposed to appear, parents took extreme care to prohibit their children from leaving the house.

Cihuacoatl, the mythical mother of the human race, painted as a serpent-woman, bearer of twins, was the goddess of fertility and reproduction.

Chalchihuitlicue was the goddess of water, and a sister of the Tlalocs. Being also a goddess of the streams and the sea, she counted among her most devoted worshipers the water-seers, fishermen, and seafarers, and all others who obtained their maintenance from the water. She was connected with the waters high in the heavens, and thus, was also regarded as a sky goddess. Among her many other attributes, she was a provider of herbs for healing purposes, and a protector of newborn babies, through "baptism," at the birth rites.

Coatlicue, mother of Huitzilopochtli, obviously was a fertility goddess, because in the spring festival held in her honor, flowers and green corn were the usual offering, the celebration of which ended in song and dance. She was greatly revered by flower-sellers.

Mictlantecultli, was lord of death and the underworld Mictlan, land of dark-ness. Mictlan was not conceived as a place of punishment; rather it was a place of habitation for those dead who had not made the grade as warriors.

Mixcoatl, god of the morning star, and the chase, seems to have been none other than Huitzilopochtli under another name, in his capacity as hunting god.

Xipe Totec was the patron divinity of the silversmiths, and his festival, which was attended with particularly bloody rites, was observed in the first month of the calendar.

Xiuhtecutli, sometimes referred to as Heuhuetectl, or "lord of turquoise," was the oldest of the gods, the great deity of fire and the household fireside, revered for his benefits; for bringing warmth; for heating and cooking.

Tonatiuh was the sun god, powerful and bloodthirsty, a patron of the preda-tory warriors and nobles whose main occupation was to provide victims for sacri-fice so that agricultural crops would not suffer. It was believed that his youth must be continuously renewed by human sacrifice so that he might continue his daily pilgrimage across the sky.

Centectl and Chicomecoatl, gods of maize, were dependent, to a great extent, on the Tlalocs, for it was only with their help that they thrived. Chicomecoatl was the goddess of food and drink, and Centectl, "heart of the earth," was the goddess of medicine and medicinal herbs. She was revered by physicians and sur-geons, by those who bled people, and also by midwives and those who gave herbs for abortions; by soothsayers who told the good or bad fortune children were going to have, according to the date, time, or signs, accompanying their birth.

She was also worshiped by all those who possessed baths, or temazcallis, in their homes, "all of whom placed the image of their goddesses in their baths, call-ing her Temazcalteci, meaning "grandmother of the baths."

Tlacaltectl, an earth and maize goddess, was also the goddess of sexual intercourse, confession, and purification. It was to her priests that adulterers would come to confession, for it was believed that confession would absolve one from his or her crime, and from the punishment ordained for the sin.

Xochiquetzal, goddess of flowers, pleasure, song and dance, representative of all revelry, was perhaps another name for Tlacaltectl, with some added characteristics. As "goddess of love," Xochiquetzal was also a goddess of "irregular" sexual pleasure, and the patroness of the prostitutes and concubines who lived with the bachelors of the military schools, the Telpuchcalli.

Thus, as patroness of these moqui or entremetides who accompanied the warriors at dances and on the field, Xochiquetzal stood as a counterpart to Tezcatlipoca, lord of the bachelor's house.

The confusing multiplicity of gods, the countless religious festivals, and the scores of temples and holy edifices necessitated a large and carefully organized priestly class. One such existed, recruited largely from the younger sons of the nobility.

In addition to the large tribal temples with their accompanying priestly set-up, every calpulli possessed its own temple and priests. Perhaps as many as five thousand priests were attached in some way to the great temple of Huitzilopochtli. The priesthood was tremendous both in numbers and influence. It could scarcely be any other way with a people of such religious fervor as the ancient Aztecs.

At the apex of the carefully organized priestly hierarchy, two pontiffs of equal standing and honor, one of whom bore the title Quetzalcoatl Totectlamacasqui, and served as the high priest of the cult of Huitzilopochtli, the Aztec war-lord. The other, who shared the same high authority, was the chief of the priestly cult of Tlaloc, god of rain, and possessed the latter's name, Tlaloctlamacazqui.

These two high priests were elected by the ruler, and all the foremost men of the tribe, on the basis of piety and wisdom, and for having performed faithfully all the customs, rules, exercises, and teachings practiced by the ministers of the temples.

Certain degrees of standing had to be attained, however, before the eligibility to these highest positions could be established. In this election, little attention was paid was paid to lineage, though they might be of the lowest extraction; instead, their probity and great knowledge of everything connected with the ceremonies of their religion was prized the most.

Immediately below them was a priest who was called the Mexicatlotenoatzin, comparable to a patriarch, who was chosen by the two highest priests. He was a supervisor of many other lesser priests and acted in the manner of a rector.

Their function was to see that everything related to the divine cult should be carried out with the proper care and perfection, in keeping with the laws and practices of the two pontiffs, particularly with respect to the education of the youths trained in the Calmecac, the temple tribal school for the children of the nobility and well-to-do.

The education in the Calmecac was primarily religious in nature, and the office of the chief administrator was regarded with great significance, since the possessor would be held accountable for the correct development of the coming generation of civil and religious leaders.

Continuing with the enumeration of the ecclesiastical hierarchy, we find two coadjutors of the Mexicatlotencatzin, one of whom had the same duties and was called Uitznahuacteohuatzin. The other was called Tepantechuatzin, and had the special duty of keeping watch over those who were educated in the monasteries.

Those priests who offered instruction to all the singers who had to appear in the temples, were called Umetoahitzin.

The Epcoaquacuiltzin supervised the festivals of the calendar, and all rites which were to come about, without any upset. He was in effect, a master of ceremonies.

The Tlapizcatzin was an instructor whose particular job it was to teach, direct, and improve the songs which were to be sung in honor of the gods at all the festivals.

Alongside of him was the Epceacuacuillitecpictoton, who composed new songs that were needed in the temples and private homes.

There were also priests of warrior rank, who presumably offered military instruction in the Calmecac to those sons of the nobility who had manifested their inclination for the profession of war. All those priests who had performed some brave deed in war, and had captured three or four prisoners, were called Tlamacastequioaque. Those who had taken captive only one in war, were called Tlamacasquecuicanime or priest-singers.

There were others who taught particular activities such as the reading and writing of hieroglyphics, oratory, tradition, lore, numbers, astronomy, astrology, chronology, geography, history, mythology, poetry, music, songs, dances, games, principles of government, tribal law, divination and religion.

With the subsequent rise of the priestly class, there came about a division of their duties, each of which demanded its own special individual training and preparation, and led to an apprenticeship for the junior priests, under senior supervision.

The Moloncotenhac were responsible for the preparation of necessities such as copal, paper, etc. for the moment of sacrifice, or the offerings before the gods on the festival of Chicunanecatl.

The Ciuteutzin had the same duties, preparing everything necessary, however, for the festival of Xilonne. The Chalchiuhtliyoucactohalquacuilli had to provide the offerings that were needed for those whom they killed during the festival of Chalchiuhliyoue, such as ulli (gum), copal, etc.

The Tzapatlatenhoatzin and Xipecopicotenhoa also had similar duties, for the festivals of Tepeilhuitl, and the sacrifices for Tequitzin. Then there were those who guarded the temples, the Tecpantzincotenhoa and the Tlalcalquaquilli, so that no irreverence should be committed there. Minor duties included the obtaining of the offerings that were to be made in respective temples.

The Ixcocahuquitzonmolcotenhoa had charge of bringing in the firewood used in the monastery called Tzommalcocalmecac. There were priests whose duties were to prepare the candlewood to make large torches, as well as red ochre, ink, sandals, jackets and small marine-shells; priests who obtained festival wine; priests whose duties it was to assemble the youths called Cuecueztteca, who were to fast in the suburb of Atempan; and a multitude of others with just as many different duties. Boys who served as sacristans were known as Tlamacatotan, or tiny ministers.

The Aztecs also included as priests, some who were musicians, and who blew horns, shells, and various other instruments.

Before entering into an account of the education which the children of the upper classes received in the Calmecac, it may be useful to glimpse some their early education at home.

For example, this is the method that the kings and nobles followed in raising their children. When their mothers or governesses had raised them for some six or seven years, and the children began to display too much liberty, they were entrusted to several tutors, with whom they were to play and amuse themselves. The mothers ordered these domestics not to permit the children to indulge in any kind of dishonesty or other antisocial action, when they went into the streets or roads.

These tutors trained their pupils to express themselves in words always polite, in proper language. Further, they were taught to be disrespectful to no one, to treat with deference all those they met, state employees, captains or hidalgos, or important people, not to mention the elderly, man or woman, even if they were of low rank.

If a person of humble position would greet the child, he or she would be taught to bow, and return the greeting, saying, "May God lead you, my good grandfather." To which the man addressed might answer, "My grandson, precious stone and rich plume, thou hast done me honor; continue thy road in good fortune." Those who would hear the child speak in this way might be expected to say, "If that child lives, he will be very noble, for he is generous; he will certainly deserve a high position."

The tutors had every motivation to acquit themselves well. It has been written that tutors who did not give a good account of the estates of their pupils, were hanged without possibility of pardon.

Those children who were foreordained by their parents to the service of the temples from their birth because of some special promise, or through a promise made to the gods during illness in exchange for preservation of life, or later, so that they might be guaranteed a happy marriage, or for the good fortune of the family, made their entrance into the religious school of the particular god to which they were dedicated, at the age of five or seven.

The sons of noblemen were generally promised however, to the Calmecac, for admission in their tenth or twelfth year. Those who were destined for the priesthood remained in the temple for their entire lives, where they would live in candor, humility, and chastity, to flee absolutely the carnal sins, and dedicate themselves to the service of the gods, while those who were inclined to matters of war, began to receive military instruction at the age of fifteen, and by twenty went off to war with their fathers and tutors.

It has long been thought that the parents of the middle classes had the liberty of selecting either the Calmecac or the Telpuchcalli for their children, although a class distinction existed between the two colleges. What should be remembered though is that it was not impossible for a middle-class student to attend the Calmecac, especially if he intended to remain for life as a priest.

Since the number of Calmecac religious schools were limited, the establishment was enclosed within certain buildings of the main temple of the various provinces. The most important of these colleges or seminaries was attached to the principle temple in Tenochtitlan, Hutizilopochtli. It was set up in the heart of the lake town, between the immense pyramid of the greater temple, and its encircling wall, adorned with figures of serpents, and a short distance from the ranks of vertical posts on which the skulls of the sacrificed victims were impaled, forming an immense covering of heads.

Any lord, principle leader, or wealthy man, whenever he offered his son to the House of the Calmecac, ordered a fine repast to be prepared, to which he invited the priests and ministers of the idols who were called Tlamacazque and Quaquaouilti, and old patricians in charge of the district. After the feast, the old men made a speech to the priests and ministers of the idols, who educated the boys, similar to what follows:

"Gentlemen, priests, ministers of our gods, you who have taken the trouble to come here to our home, and our lord almighty who brought you—we make it known unto you that it pleased the lord to favor us by giving us a child like jewel. We hope to deserve that this boy may be reared and live, and as it is a male child, it is not suitable for us to assign to him women's duties, and thus keep him in the home. Therefore we give him to you, as your son, and recommend him to you now at this moment.

"We offer him to the lord Quetzalcoatl, or by another name, Tilpotonqui, that he may enter the house of the Calmecac, which is a house of penance and tears, where the nobles are reared.

"For it is the place where they treasures of god are attained through prayer and doing penance with tears and signs; and entreating god to be merciful and favor them with his treasures, we offer him to you so that when he reaches the required age, he may enter and live in the house of our lord, where the nobles are brought up and educated; and that this our son be in charge of the sweeping and cleaning of the house of the lord.

"We therefore humbly entreat you to receive and take him as your own son, that he may enter and live with the other ministers of our gods in that house where by day and night all the exercises of penance are held, such as crawling on knees and elbows, praying, entreating, weeping and sighing before our lord."

The priests and ministers replied to the parents of the boy in the following manner:

"We have listened to your address, although we are unworthy to hear it, stating that you wish your beloved son, your precious gem, enter and live in the house of the Calmecac. It is not to us that this entreaty should be made; rather, you should make it to the lord Quetzalcoatl, in whose name we heard it. To him it is that you should speak; he knows what it will be his pleasure to do with your precious son, and with you, his parents. We, therefore, his unworthy servants, await with uncertainty what his pleasure is. We do not know at this time, but hope in the almighty lord to dispose as to what will be his pleasure to do with this youth."

It was then the custom to take the boy and carry him to the house of the Calmecac. The boy's parents took papers, incense, and belts with them, as well as gold bead-strings and precious stones, to place before the statue of Quetzalcoatl.

Upon reaching it, they painted the boy's body and face with ink, and put wood beads, called Tlacopatli around his neck. If he was the son of poor people, they used loose cotton strings. Then they pierced his ears to extract blood, which they offered before the statue of Quetzalcoatl.

It was then the custom for the father of the child to introduce him formally to the teachers who were to raise him. His words were to meant to convey the following sentiments:

"My son, here you are arrived in the house where our lord is everywhere. Your father and mother who bore you have brought you here. Although it is true that you owe your existence to your father and mother, it is even more true that your real fathers are those who must raise you, who must teach you good habits and must open your eyes and ears so that you truly see and hear. They have the authority to punish, to hurt and scold.

"Listen well now, and know that when you were at the most tender age, your mother and father made a vow to offer you so that you live in this house of Calmecac, in order to sweep and clean, for love of our lord Quetzalcoatl. We come to put you in this place to stay hereafter.

"Listen well my beloved child, you were born and live in this world where our lord sent you. When you were born, you were not as you are now; you could neither walk nor talk, nor do anything. Your mother brought you up; she suffered for you many a hardship; she watched over you when you slept; she cleaned the dirt from your body and fed you with her milk.

"And now, although you are young, you grow already in height and intelligence; you are going to enter this place called Calmecac where your father and mother made a vow to place you, an institution of tears and sadness whose pupils are cut and pierced like precious stones; and you will sprout here and flower like a rose.

"You will serve without cease our lord, who rewards with his mercy. You will rise to govern, with kings, senators, nobles who administer the country. From here come those who possess the high posts of the state, where they are placed and kept in order by our lord, who is everywhere. Here rise also those who are in military positions and who have the power of giving death and shedding blood. It is for these reasons that it is fitting, my beloved child, that you enter here willingly, and keep no attachment for the things of your home.

"Do not think to yourself, "My mother and father are still living; my other relatives are also living; everything is abundant, and flourishes in the house where I was born." Do not remember any of these things. Listen well to what you must do. You will have to sweep, to pick up the sweepings, to keep in order the things which are in the house; you will get up in the morning, you will stay up during the night, you will do what you are ordered to do, and you will accept the employ which is given to you. If it is necessary to jump or to run to do anything at all, you will run or jump.

"You will walk briskly; you will be neither slow nor lazy; do instantly what you are ordered to do; when you are called, you will respond with eagerness. Even when it is not you they are addressing, go running to the place where they are calling, and do yourself what you know is wanted; hurry always to carry out what is commanded.

"Notice well, my child, that you are not going there to be honored, obeyed and esteemed; but to be ordered, humiliated, scorned and abased. If your body wishes to fly into a passion and take too much control, punish it, humiliate it, and lose all memory of carnal desires. If by chance you permit some bad and unclean thought to enter your heart, you would lose all the worth and indulgence that the lord has shown you. So it is proper that you make every possible effort to stifle all your desires for sensuality and revolt. You must every day cut thorns of "maguey" to do penance and bouquets to decorate the altars. You will also have to bleed your body with thorns and bathe every night even if it is very cold.

"Take care not to fill your stomach too much when eating; be temperate; practice fasting. Those who are thin and have only skin on their bones don't have a body that aspires to carnal things; if desire comes sometimes, is passes quickly like an attack of fever. Don't cower under too many covers; do not put on heavy clothes; so that your body may harden under the influence of the cold. In truth, you are going to do penance, ask for indulgence from our lord, aspire to his riches, partake of his treasures. In time of fasting, do not break it; do like the others; see in it nothing irritating; practice resolutely fasting and penitence.

"You must strive to understand the books of our lord. Stay near the wise men and the men who are learned and of good character. You are already intelligent and discreet; you are no longer an infant. You will be told many things here, for great truths are said here. It is to those lessons given by old men that you will add those your heard from your mother and father. Listen then: if ever you are told something you do not understand, do not laugh at it. Never forget this. If you were to laugh at it, you will be forever unhappy. Listen well to your elders."

Upon the entrance of the youths into the Calmecac, they were greeted by music rendered by older students on sacred shells and resonant drums called Teponaxtlis. The festivities did not last long, however.

Some of the duties enforced upon these young boys entailed drilling in monastic discipline, and the performance of such acts as bringing firewood from the forests for the temple fires, maguey thorns, laurel branches for adorning the shrines of the gods, tending the sacred fires, and participating in religious festivals.

They had to prepare the ink with which the priests blackened their bodies everyday. In addition to blackening their bodies with ink, the priests rubbed their bodies with a mixture of poisonous insects such as scorpions, spiders and worms, and even small serpents. This mixture was first burned in the temple. The ashes were then beaten in a mortar, together with some ink made of the foot of ocatl, tobacco and herb, and additional live insects.

With this anointment, the priests felt themselves fearless to any danger whatsoever, calling it Teopatli, also deeming it a powerful remedy for several disorders. The young boys new to the seminaries were specifically charged with the collecting of such little animals and insects; and being accustomed at an early age to that kind of employment, they soon lost the horror which attends the first familiarity with such insects and reptiles.

The young boys were also taught to speak well, to conduct themselves courteously and modestly, to count, to sing sacred songs, to dance, and something of their Aztec astrology. They aided the priests in their daily religious rites, in their incense offerings, and in their charities. Physical hardships were also imposed upon them in preparation for their later more exacting duties.

Those sons of the well-to-do who entered the Calmecac at the usual age of ten or twelve, performed similar temple duties, and also were taught the traditions of their fathers, arithmetic, the art of picture-writing and reading, astronomical and calendrical matters, and astrology, principles of law and government, music and dance, and such natural history and science as were known by the Aztecs at that time.

After several years, usually at the age of fifteen, those students who inclined naturally to the matters of the temple, and who were deemed destined to be ecclesiastical men, were drawn out of the college and placed in the temple, in the lodgings appointed for religious men; they were then given to the various religious orders, whose prelates and masters would thereafter teach them that which concerned their future religious profession.

Similarly, those students of the Calmecac who were inclined to the wars, upon reaching maturity were turned over to the military priests for adult instruction.

Those intended for civil offices began their apprenticeship in the respective government divisions, similar to the training we have already discussed in connection with the judiciary.

Education in the religious schools of the Calmecac always exhibited the same characteristics as those seen in the breeding at home. Above all, they endeavored to make one's will control the "bodily appetites:" to conquer pain by resisting it; to triumph over hunger, exhaustion, inclement weather, sleep, physical defects, and to develop the hardiest souls in the strongest bodies.

For these reasons, food was limited, sleeping facilities very crude, garb poor, repose brief. Long trips were made, and repentances were ever-recurring.

Fastings were carried to the extreme. It was a common occurrence in the asceticism that the Mexican priests practiced. Fasting is one of the most general and ancient forms of adoration. It rests on an instinctive feeling that a man is more worthy to present himself before the divine beings when fasting than when stuffed with food. In addition, fasting is shown by experience to promote dreams, hallucinations, ecstasies, which have always been considered as so many forms of communication with the deity.

Customs observed in the Calmecac were broken down to specific customs or rules:

The first was that all ministers of the idols who were called Tlamacazque, were to sleep in the House of Calmecac.

The second rule was that they all swept and cleaned that house at four o'clock in the morning.

The third was that the bigger boys had to go out and look for and gather maguey thorns.

The fourth was for still older boys to bring in firewood on their backs from the forest. This wood was needed for the fires which were lighted every night; and when any construction work in clay was to be done, be it building walls, ditches, watering canals, or field work, they all went together to work at daybreak, only those who had to watch the house, and those who had to carry the food to the workers, remaining. No one was ever permitted to lag behind, and they all worked with great discipline and good order.

The fifth rule was to stop work somewhat early; they then went at once to their monastery to bathe, be in charge of the services of their gods, and to perform penance exercises. At sunset they began to get all of the necessary things ready, then at eleven o'clock at night they went on their way, each one alone by himself, naked, carrying the thorns of maguey, a shell on which to play a tune on the road, an incensory of clay, a pouch or bag in which to carry incense, and a torch.

Each young man thus went out naked to deposit the maguey thorns at his particular place of devotion, and those who wanted to do severe penance went far towards the forests, mountains and rivers.

The older boys would go as far as half a league from the monastery to deposit the maguey thorns and do penance rituals.

The sixth rule was that meals were consumed had to be prepared in the house of the Calmecac, because they had a communal income which they spent on food.

The seventh rule was that every midnight, all had to get up to pray, and he who did not awake and rise was punished by pricking him with maguey thorns in the ears, chest, thighs and legs, in the presence of all the ministers of the idols so that he might take warning.

The eighth rule was that no one should be overbearing or offensive, nor should anyone be disobedient to the order and customs they observed; and if at one time or another, one of them appeared intoxicated, or should live in concubinage, or commit some criminal act, they killed him outright, executed him with garrote, roasted him alive, or shot arrows at him. If anyone committed a venal sin, they pierced his ears and sides with thorns and an awl.

The ninth rule demanded that all the ministers of the idols were to bathe at midnight.

The tenth rule ordained that when there was a fasting day, the youngest as well as the oldest had to observe the fast until at least noon; and when it was one of the fasts called Atamalqualc, they fasted until the subsequent midnight. Still others ate only once at noon, but at night never tasted a thing, not even water.

The eleventh rule ordained that the boys must speak well, bow, and stand up immediately in the presence of their elders.

The twelfth rule was to teach the boys all the verses of the songs to sing, which they called divine songs. Further, they had to learn the counting of years, interpretation of dreams, and astrology.

The thirteenth rule was that the ministers of the idols had to make their vow to live chastely without ever knowing a woman carnally, to eat abstemiously, not to tell lies, and to live devoutly in fear of god.

These junior priests were held up as models to the community. As a testimony of their penance and of their praying for the people, they would present to view on the parapets of the temple, their blood-covered bodies, stained from their personal sacrifice.

It makes one shudder to learn of the austerities which they exercised upon themselves, either in atonement of their transgressions, or in preparation for their festivals. They literally mangled their flesh as if it had been insensible, and let their blood run in such profusion that it appeared to be a superfluous part of the body. It was not only the priesthood however, who drew blood from the body, but all persons, young and old, did it frequently, as an act of individual devotion to the gods.

The priests were sticklers for the proper performance of ritual, and exacted a severe punishment from all who committed a breach. At the beginning of the rainy season which occurred towards the end of May, a great fast was kept for the rain god, Tlaloc, for the purpose of obtaining a plentiful rainfall to hasten the growth of the crops just then on the point of germinating.

This fast was observed with rigid exactness by the whole body of priests, including the very youngest. Throughout this fast, great caution was taken to prevent the committing of the smallest trespass or improper act.

The priests and students were obliged to see that not the slightest bit of dust was to fall on their garments, nor to err one whit in the carrying out of the ceremonies. The officiating ministers were not supposed to falter in any manner on the way to the functions. On the last day before the main feast, all those who had committed some fault were punished severely, as expiation of their misdeeds, and to propitiate the violent anger of the gods.

Blowing their trumpets and shells, they started in procession to lead all those who had committed a mistake or fault during the ceremonies of the fast to the designated place where punishment was to be meted out to them. To prevent their escape, the adults were conducted like prisoners, held by the hair of the neck, or their waists, and the little boys, or sacristans, carried on shoulders. Still other boys, a little older, were held by the hand.

They took them to the water, (lake) where they were to be punished. All along the way, wherever they found some pool of water, they would throw the prisoners in, ill-treating them with kicks and blows; they would roll them in the mud or slime of any water-hole, until they reached the banks of the lake they called Toteco.

Upon reaching the shore of that lake, the high priest and his ministers first burnt paper and incense. At the same time, the prisoners were thrust into the water, and the blows produced a great noise. If any of them scampered out of the water, they ducked them again. Those who could not swim fared very badly, for they were ducked time and again until they were left for dead on the edge of the banks.

The procession then worked its way back to the temple, with the exception that now the chastised children and youths went home with their relatives to recuperate, bruised, trembling with cold, teeth chattering.

This method of chastisement would seem to bear out the idea that terror, not love, was the spring of education with the Aztecs.

The instruction in religion and the arts and sciences must have been of an advanced and esoteric nature, with specializations that produced priest-astrologers, priest-astronomers, priests for sacrifices, priest-historians, and so forth.

Turning to the education of the daughters of the upper classes, we find that some received their training at home from the age of four onwards, and never made an appearance in public until shortly before their marriage. The times they went to the temple were few in number, and then only because of a vow or some other particular circumstance. From their childhood, they were taught the household feminine duties of spinning, weaving, and cooking, and were kept occupied constantly.

They were never permitted to dine in the presence of men, even brothers, until they were married. Furthermore, they maintained a deep silence during meals. Their quarters were kept widely apart from those of the men, and they were always under the close supervision of governesses.

It was usual, however, for most of the girls of the well-to-do to enter the Calmecac at the age of twelve or thirteen, for a period of two to three years; some remained until marriage, while others took a perpetual vow, and remained for life.

The priesthood was not limited to men only, and these latter girls, after serving apprenticeship in the seminaries, were also permitted to participate in the intimate services of the temple. Their duties were minor, such as proffering incense to the idols, looking after the sacred fires, sweeping, and making ready the food which they offered to the images every day with their own hands. They were, however, completely barred from the high distinction of sacrificing, and the higher ranks of the priestly order.

It was a usual occurrence for the parents, immediately upon the birth of the girl, to offer her to the order of some particular god, such as Tezcatlipoca, and to notify the rector of that area concerning it. He in turn informed the Tepantlehuatzin, who was the superior general of the seminaries.

They brought her to the temple two months later, and presented her to the priest in charge, who was similar to a curate. In her small hands were placed a small broom and a little clay vessel (for burning incense) with some copal in it, to make evident to all her destination. This visit occurred once every month, and each time, the bark of trees, copal, and brooms were brought along as an offering for the sacred fire.

When the child was older, she had to learn how to sing and dance, so that she could take part in the service of the gods called Moyocoya, Tezcatlipoca, and Yactl. Although she belonged to this convent, she continued to stay with her father and mother until she was twelve or thirteen.

At the day of her installation into the temple, a banquet was given to the oldest nuns of the convent. They received the child formally, presenting her to the god Quetzalcoatl, to whose service the house was dedicated. They spoke to their god in the following terms:

"Oh lord, protector of us all! Here are these vassals who bring to you a new servant, offered by her parents so that she may remain attached to your service. You know well the little one who belongs to you. May it please you to receive her so that she may sweep and decorate for some time your house of penitence and tears, where the daughters of the nobility come to join in your riches, praying to you and acclaiming you with greatest devotion; and in the midst of their tears, without ever ceasing to ask that they may be inspired by your words and your virtues, may you desire, oh lord, to honor her with your favors, and to receive her.

"Allow her to enter in the company of the virgins called tlamacazquo, who do penance, serve in the temple, and cut their hair. Oh lord, protector of us all, may you act towards here according to your divine will, by granting to her the favors that you know befit her."

Then, the nuns spoke to the girls in the following terms:

"Beloved little ones, here are your parents who bore you, and who vowed when you were small, to offer you to our lord who is everywhere, so that you would become one of the perfect sisters of his divine majesty. They made the offering of your person so that you may enter and live with the nuns of calmecac. And now that you have reached the age of reason, I beg of you to fulfill with all your heart the vows which they made for you.

"Do not break these vows! You are entering into the home of god, where they acclaim him and worship him. This is a place of devotion, where our lord divides his riches with his servants, whose lives are filled with his gifts. It is here that one seeks and begs for his affection and love through penitence. In this place, she who cries, sighs with devotion, humiliates herself and draws near to our lord, does herself a great favor, because our lord will laden her with gifts and adorn her with his graces. God indeed scorns and repulses nobody. It is, on the contrary, she who scorns and disdains the service of our lord who digs herself into the abyss. Our lord will punish her by sending decay to her body, blindness to her eyes, or some other sickness, to that she may be miserable in this life. Poverty, afflictions, and the greatest misfortunes will dwell with her.

"It is for these reasons by beloved daughters, that I advise you to go willingly and in peace to join the virgin sisters of our lord, called sisters of penitence, to cry with devotion in this holy place. This is what you must do and observe: you will never bear either in your thoughts or in your heart anything carnal; your will, your desire, your heart must be like precious sapphire; you must force your heart and body to forget all pleasures of the flesh. "You will also take the greatest care to always sweep and keep proper the house of our lord; you will devote your cares to the dishes and drinks of our lord who is everywhere.

"It is true that our lord has no need for eating and drinking like mortals; but he accepts it as an offering; and so you will have to take charge with zeal the grinding and preparing the drink of cocoa in order to offer it to the lord.

"Take care to be obedient; don't wait to be called twice. For it is in sound learning, progress in virtue, reverence, fear of god, humility and peace that you will come to possess true nobility and greatness.

"Take care, my daughter, not to be dissolute, shameless or flighty. Let the others live as they will; imitate neither their bad example, nor their bad habits; put all your zeal to coming nearer to our lord; call him; raise your voices to him with real devotion.

"You will not be asked to give a full account of what others do in this world; you must account only for your own deeds, no matter what others will have done."

Immediately upon the entrance of the girls into the seminary, within the inner courts of the temple, all of their hair was cut off. They were informed however, that it would later be permitted to grow back, as was the Aztec custom. There they dwelled most virtuously, in silence and seclusion, under the watchful eyes of their superiors, without any verbal discourse with men.

They all spent the night in one dormitory, and slept with their clothes on so that they might always be ready for labor when they were made to arise. It was the duty of several to rise about two hours before midnight, some others at midnight, and sill others at dawn, to keep the fires alive and make incense offerings to the idols.

Even in the fulfillment of this duty, though they met with the priests, they were segregated from them under the watch of the matron superiors, to avert the occurrence of any possible disturbance.

Every morning they cleaned the temples, and got the provisions in readiness which formed the daily food offering to the idols. In the intervals when they were not employed in religious activities, they were engaged in learning various feminine occupations, particularly spinning, weaving and embroidering rich and beautiful cloths for the altars, and the adorning of the sanctuaries.

It was this advanced domestic training, as well as their being virgins, which made these girls, when graduated, valued, respected, and desirable as brides. Nothing was more zealously guarded than the purity of these virgins. Any voluntary or involuntary transgression was unforgivable. If it was kept undiscovered, the guilty girl made efforts to placate the wrath of the gods by penitence's, fasting, and strict conduct, because she feared that as punishment for her sin, her flesh would rot.

During certain particular days of penance, the girls in the religious seminaries of the Calmecac would pierce the upper part of their ears with maguey thorns and put the drawn blood on their cheeks as a religious rouge; then they would bathe in a designated basin, set aside for the purpose. They were called upon frequently to assist at religious festivals and dances, their feet and hands dressed with feathers. Their conduct was constantly under watch, and every precaution was taken to see that they were not molested.

When they reached the age of sixteen or eighteen, they had the alternative of remaining in the temple for the rest of their lives as priestesses, or of marrying, which latter was the usual decision.

There was very little courtship done among the Aztecs. The marriages were customarily arranged by the parents. After the latter had succeeded in obtaining a prospective husband, they offered to the superior general of the seminary a certain number of quails, and a certain amount of copal, flowers and food.

In addition, the girls' parents made a formal speech in which they expressed their gratitude for the care and consideration the superior general had displayed in the education of their daughter, and at this time, requested his consent to arrange the marriage. The superior general complied with the petition in his formal reply, admonishing the pupil to a constancy in virtue, and the carrying out of all the duties that marriage entailed.

The termination of the festival held during the fifth month, in honor of the great god Tezcatlipoca, marked the dismissal from the seminaries of all the young men and women whose years of service in the temples were over, and who had reached the suitable age for marriage.

As the ceremonies drew to a close, a culmination was attained when the victim representing the god Tezcatlipoca was sacrificed. The victim selected was the most handsome and well-formed of all the prisoners. At the close of the ceremony of the same festival held the previous year, the youth had been chosen, and for the whole year following, he went about dressed constantly in an outfit resembling that worn by the divinity.

Conditions were made pleasant for him, but it was during his last month before the festival that he tasted to the utmost all the pleasures of life. He was married to four beautiful virgins, and on the last five days, he was entertained lavishly.

On the last day of the festival, he was led, along with a large following, to the temple of Tezcatlipoca. He accompanied the idol of the god in the procession, and when the hour of sacrifice approached, they stretched him upon the altar, and the high priest, with great reverence, opened his chest and pulled out his heart.

His body was not, like the bodies of the other victims, thrown down the stairs; instead, it was carried in the arms of the priests, and beheaded at the bottom of the temple. His head was strung up in the Tzompantli, among the rest of the skulls of the victims sacrificed to Tezcatlipoca, and his legs and arms dressed and prepared for the tables of the lords.

After the sacrifice, a grand dance took place for the collegiate youths and nobles present. At sunset, the virgins of the temple made a new offering of bread, baked with honey, put before the altar of Tezcatlipoca, and destined to be the reward of the youths who should be the victors in the race down the temple stairs; they were also rewarded with a garment, and received the praise and applause of the spectators.

The festival was concluded by dismissing from the seminaries all the youths and virgins who were arrived at an age fit for marriage. The youths who remained, mocked the others, throwing at them handfuls of flowers, upbraiding them for leaving the service of god for the pleasures of matrimony, the priests always granting them indulgence in this exuberant display.

6

The Military

No profession was held in more esteem among the Aztecs than the profession of arms. Economically, a large proportion of their prosperity was based on the tribute exacted from their exploited neighbors, and from this source came much of their sustenance.

Conquest by means of war meant slaves to help in the fields, in the erection of temples, pyramids, buildings, canals and bridges. Successful wars paved the way for merchants, opened new markets for them, and extended the limits in which they could trade.

The rise to great political power of the Aztecs from their former position of subjugation in the Valley of Mexico was due to their military prowess and achievement, and the people were aware of this factor. Correspondingly, their custom of granting awards and honors in recognition of military accomplishments was establishing a social hierarchy which would desire to continue the glorification of war.

The awards often included new lands to be tilled, with aid coming from the surrounding peoples, or they took the form of promotion to higher ranks with an increasing display of personal marks of distinction, such as insignia, costly or elaborate clothing, artistic feather headdresses or jewelry.

Ever closely linked with their religion, war, and the deity of war, was the most revered by them and regarded as the chief protector of the nation. In affairs of state, election to the highest offices, and leadership of the tribe, could be attained only by the possession of youth, characteristics of the highest bravery, fitness for and skill in war, and the taking of delight and glory therein.

No prince was elected king until he had in several battles displayed proofs of his courage and military skill, and merited the splendid post of general of the army. No king was crowned until he had taken with his own hands the victims which were to be sacrificed at the festival of his coronation.

The Aztecs were convinced that only by making sacrificial offerings of the hearts of men could the strength of the gods be maintained; also, their benevolence depended upon lavish human sacrifice, and these offerings were most generally to be obtained in war. The speech made by the high priest at the anointment of the newly-elected ruler states this clearly:

"You are the one to direct and give orders in matters of war; see to it that you give much care to this; you have to watch carefully in making the sun come to earth. You must labor that there shall be no lack of blood and food for the sun-god, because he must be well treated in his course to supply us with light, and for the goddess of the earth as well so she gives us our sustenance; and look well that you watch overt the punishment and death of the wicked, even of the lords, and those disobedient and delinquent."

Then too, as the festive celebration of installing the tribal leader drew to a close, the latter would, in keeping with custom, loudly proclaim war against the enemies of the tribe. This was done to demonstrate the greatness of their dominion in war.

To this end, they at once chose the most valiant men and strongest warriors, and all those who considered themselves as such approached the chief in competition, for each wished to be the one selected for such activity. This not only afforded them an opportunity to show themselves worthy of the honor, and give them a means of livelihood, but it also credited them with the desire to die in battle. Those who died for the sake of their country in battle, weapons in hand, were imagined to be the happiest souls in the afterlife, where they went to a heaven to live with the lord in glory and joy for all eternity, and sipped the sweetness of flowers, where there was no night and day, no year and no time, but only enjoyment and splendor without end.

All of the above contributed to make war assume a dominant role in the lives of the Aztecs, and as a result of their desire to take living captives for the purposes of sacrifice, they adopted military tactics the aim of which was to fight skillfully, but not necessarily to kill.

Ultimately, this may have been the source of their downfall before the hands of the Conquistadors. This particular custom of the Aztecs contributed in no small manner to the success of the Spanish Conquistadors, because in the early days of their campaign, it saved them many times from instant death and complete annihilation.

This attitude colored the whole of Aztec policy towards the surrounding peoples with whom they came in contact. They made no attempt to weld the neighboring tribes into a solid empire, for that, if successful, would have brought peace. In the days of their greatest power they exercised no more than a loose sovereignty over the dependent cities, which were left very much to their own devices, provided that they were punctual in the payment of tribute.

This lack of political control almost encouraged revolt; and revolt on the part of a tributary was by no means unwelcome to the Aztecs, since it afforded them an opportunity of obtaining more victims for sacrifice.

From the great esteem in which the profession of arms was held amongst them, the Aztecs placed great store in making their children courageous, and to inure them from their earliest infancy to the hardships of war. This last statement is vividly portrayed when we recall how the future duties of the son of a soldier were symbolized in the baptismal rites, with the placing alongside the baby a small bow and four arrows.

Since it was required of every adult member of the tribe to be prepared to respond to the call to arms, physical development was begun at a very early stage of the boy's life, by means of play, work, and apprenticeship in some industrial occupation.

The actual training for warriorhood in the skillful use of weapons was acquired through hunting and fishing, in the chase both on land and water, when the father taught the boy to use bow and arrow, dart and javelin, all of which served as an excellent means of preparation for the later vigorous and exacting duty of war.

Boys of six, coming from the middle-classes, made up of the smaller merchants, petty chieftains, and property-holding agricultural masses, could be delivered to special priests and warriors for education in the seminary attached to the local calupulli temple. The parents generally waited, however, until their sons reached the age of ten or twelve before entering them. These schools were distinguished by the name of Telpuchcalli, derived from telpuchtli, meaning youth, and "calli," meaning house, and were essentially training houses in which the bachelors received instruction in the profession of arms.

Even after warriorhood was achieved, they live and slept there until they married and settled in homes of their own.

Whereas the Calmecac or religious schools were under the direction of the priests and their favored god was Quetzalcoatl, the youth in the Telpuchcalli were placed under the guidance of warriors as well as priests, and their god was Tezcatlipoca.

Before the boy was given over to the Telpuchcalli, it was the custom for the parents to make arrangements for an excellent dinner, and invite as guests the teachers unto whose care their children were later to be entrusted. When the feast was drawing to a close, the father would turn to the priest-teachers, and address them in this fashion:

"Our lord, creator of heaven and earth, has brought you here to let you know that it has pleased him to grant us the favor of allowing a child, born to us, to live. It is not right that we should show him the tasks of women, keeping him in the home; therefore we give him to you as your son, and place you in charge of him, because you hold the office of raising the young men and teaching them our customs so that they may become courageous men and serve the gods Tlaltecutli and Tonantiuh, who art the earth and son, in war.

"For this reason, we offer him to the almighty god. Perhaps he will grow and live, pleasing to god; he will enter the house of penance and weeping which is called Telpouchcalli, and we turn him over to you from this moment that he may live in the house where courageous men are reared, and come forth as such, and receive the treasures of god and be granted the mercy and grace of giving them victories, so that they may become chiefs, possessing the ability to govern and rule the common people.

"And we, unworthy parents, may we by chance deserve it that our weeping and our penance should cause this boy to be reared to live and grow well to fulfill his promise? We humbly entreat you to receive and accept him as a son, that he may enter and live with the fortunate sons of chiefs, and others who are being educated in this Telpuchcalli."

As the ceremonies progressed, the teachers of the boys and young men answered in the following manner:

"We consider it a high favor to have heard your reasoning; you are addressing not us, but the lord god Iaotl, in whose representation we have listened to it. It is he to whom you speak, to whom you offer and give your son, and we receive him in his name. He alone knows what it will be his pleasure to do with him. We, his unworthy servants, await with uncertain hope what this may be, in accordance with what he had already granted as favors to suit his disposition and determination which the unknown one had decided to grant before the beginning of the world.

"In truth, we do not know the natural abilities which at that time were granted to him, as his property and standing; we also ignore what the favors might have been that he granted this boy when he was baptized. We also ignore the sign, good or bad, under which he was born and baptized, for we, his humble servants, cannot divine these things.

"In truth, we bring our good fortune with us into the world when we are born, for it was allotted to us since before the beginning of the world. We wish and pray that he may be given all the wealth due him, and wish that all the natural gifts and favors with which our lord adorned him and endowed him before the beginning of this world may manifest themselves and shine while he lives in this house.

"We do not know whether by chance god may claim him for himself by taking his life in childhood, and whether perhaps we do not deserve it that he should live a long time in this world. We know nothing for certain except to say to you in order to console you, that we cannot tell you with certainty that he will be, or that he will do, nor this will happen, or he will be extolled, or he will live on earth.

"Only the lord knows if on account of our unworthiness he will be despicable, poor, and despised on earth, or perhaps will become a thief or adulterer, or else live a hard and wretched life. We however, shall do our full duty, which is to rear and educate him like parents, but we shall be unable to enter within him and put our own heart into him; you could not do that either, notwithstanding the fact that you are his true parents. There only remains to say that we all should not fail to commend him to god in our prayers so that god may show us his will."

After having entered the Telpuchcalli, the boys were held responsible for the coarser tasks necessary for the maintenance of the temple and its services. Their duties were to sweep and clean house; bring firewood and light the numerous sacred fires and incense braziers which burned night and day in the temples; summon the people to religious services by pounding the huehuetl drums; cut the wood and draw the water necessary in the temple exercises; observe the required fasts; make up the paint with which the priests decorated themselves, splice the maguey thorns used in blood-letting, penances and sacrifices; gather rushes and green branches in all other things needed for adorning the temple at the various festive rites; and perform many other odd jobs.

The Telpuchcalli were under the special supervision of able and experienced leaders called "Speakers of the Youth," or telpuchtlatoca,. They were responsible not only for the training and instruction of the pupils in the professional use and practice of arms, but also for the development of their intellectual powers as far as the state of their knowledge allowed. The instructors held their positions throughout life, or as long as they fulfilled their duties satisfactorily.

The curriculum embraced a practical course in arts and crafts, religious instruction, a rigid moral and physical training, and instruction in songs, hymns, history and tradition. Rhythmic dancing was also looked upon as an important factor in their education, and so according to custom, at the first sign of evening, all of the youths, including novices, went to the house called cuicacalco to perform rhythmic exercises.

In the Telpuchcalli as in the Calmecac, the training of the will and firmness of character were stressed. There too, the students were compelled to undergo privations, including fasting, penances, extreme labor and cruel punishments.

Religion and warfare were so firmly allied in ancient Aztec culture that it was not uncommon to perceive the young men devoting themselves solemnly to both these callings simultaneously. When the boy in the Telpuchcalli attained his fifteenth year, his military training began in earnest, concomitantly with his general education.

Those boys of the poorer classes who had to remain home and receive their education from their parents, were delivered at age fifteen to adjutants of the local calpulli. These young men obtained their military training by going to war and learning the art of fighting in actual combat.

The students in the Telpuchcalli, having become "little fighting men," were put through tests by the older youths to determine whether they possessed the strength to be taken to war.

If they were found not wanting, they would then be taken along on the campaigns as recruits, to observe operations or carry shields and war baggage strapped on their backs. If a youth was well trained and conducted himself fittingly, and was well grounded in the required exercises, he, in turn, was appointed teacher of the novices and called Tiacucauh.

The next step up in rank came in recognition of valor and ability, and was the appointment as leader—Telpuchtlato—of all the young men in the Telpuchcalli, along with the power to mete out punishment.

The capture of four enemy warriors would result in the appointment of the youth as Tlacatecatl, or commander of a subdivision of two hundred to four hundred men. He would also be called upon to keep the peace and preserve order in public places, somewhat like a local sheriff. In this role, he would carry a large cane decorated with white feathers signifying his presence, one of unusual authority, which could bring about arrest and death.

Life in the Telpuchcalli was strict and harsh. The students slept in the college buildings attached to the temple, apart from one another in hard beds. While they were permitted to eat most of their meals at their own homes, anyone caught not returning to sleep at the Telpuchcall was punished severely.

Whenever they went out to work, it was in organized groups, never alone. For their own sustenance and the daily wants of worship, they tilled in common, certain special fields or temple-tracts; for the clergy and state they built edifices, palaces, causeways, ditches and canals. Their own interests were submerged to those of their religion and town.

A frequent task of theirs was to go forth as a unit to the forests, and return with firewood on their backs for the fires of the cuicacalco. After any sort of menial work, they would halt shortly after sundown, return to their homes to bathe, then return to school.

There they proceeded to paint with ink their whole bodies, excluding their faces, and dressed themselves in loose blankets of maguey thorns, and strings of seashell beads. Instead of combing their hair, they made it stand on end in a wild fashion, to make themselves look ferocious.

Next, they painted their faces with white pyrite; in the perforations of their ears they wore turquoise. On their heads they wore white plumes. Their superiors, their principal teachers, wore the same kind of blankets, but the shells were made of gold.

At the end of the day, all went to sleep in their respective Telpuchcalli of the different districts, and those who lived in concubinage went to sleep with their women.

While they were attending the Telpuchcalli, the drinking of wine was forbidden, except for the older students, who, however, drank little, always unseen. They never permitted themselves to appear intoxicated in public. If a youth was seen drunk in the market square, his punishment was death by garrote.

This was executed before all the young men as a warning, to instill an everlasting fear of the consequences of inebriation. If the guilty one was of noble birth, his demise was brought about secretly.

In spite of subjecting their bodies to severe penances, the young men gave major regard to the preservation and growth of their physical powers. They were given ample opportunity to exercise not only in the use of arms, but bodily, in the schools and at most religious festivals. Since their capitol, the city of Tenochtitlan, was situated on a lake, the exercise of rowing was often included.

The exercise of running was not slighted for they trained youths to serve as couriers, laboring to have them well-conditioned so that they might run to the top of a high hill without fatigue.

The schools also combined the exercise of running with that of wrestling so that the future warrior could become expert in the taking of prisoners rather than in killing them outright.

In addition to the above, there were other types of exercise, including a game of ball, called tlachtli, which was intimately associated with religion and the priesthood. In every principle village there was a tlachtli ball-court on which they played, and some of the larger towns had more than one. The courts were always constructed near the more religious temples.

The ball game tlatchli was a favorite sport of even the earlier Nahuans and Mayans. There is a story in the sacred book of Popol Vuh in which the mythological heroes of the tribe played against the gods of evil a game of tlatchli, with the stakes being nothing less than the destiny of mankind.

The Aztecs, religious to such an extent that it may be said no aspect of their personal individual or collective life was not permeated with religious emotional feelings, looked upon their exercises, games and dances not only as we of the present do, as a means of recreation and amusement, but also of having a mystical import. It seems that the performance of certain ceremonies was essential, prior to the use of the courts for playing purposes.

For example, at midnight, on a lucky day, two idols—one of the game—and one of the ball—were placed on the top of the lower walls of the ball-court with certain ceremonies and witchcraft; and in the middle of the floor they sang songs and performed ceremonies. Then a priest from the great temple came to bless the court. Certain words were said, the ball was thrown four times, and after such ceremonies the court was ordained to be consecrated and fit to be played in.

The size of the enclosed spaces which made up the ball-game courts, oriented north and south, varied. Some were as much as two hundred feet in length, and thirty feet wide. The courts were surrounded with palm trees. Walls, which made up the sides of the ball-court, were covered with smooth slabs of stone and scattered carved decorations, and were usually about fifteen feet high.

Often, these carvings were made so that a figure of Xochipilli, the patron god of games held the center ring in his arms. Two large stone rings with holes in the center extended from the center of each of the two walls, enclosing the long sides of the court.

The exact number of players varied. They did play in parties, with as few as two against two, three against three, etc. On some occasions, one city challenged another, usually with much betting on the side, the stakes ranging to as high as personal liberty.

The kings themselves often participated and offered up challenges to each other. Montezuma II of Mexico and Nezahualpilli of Tezcoco met in a famous match which was won by the latter.

The ball used in the game was made of a rubber gum substance that when molded, turned black and hardened. The players received it and hit with buttocks, haunches, and knees, the use of hands being forbidden. The participants, therefore, wore no clothes except a strip of hardened deer skin between the buttocks, and as they frequently had to support themselves with their hands on the ground, during swift maneuverings for position on the field, they also had some kind of glove (mazeuatl) on their hands fastened at the wrist.

A colored line, green or black, was scratched upon the earth dividing the court in half, marking off the ground between the two stone goal discs opposite each other. Each team was stationed along one of the widened T-shaped ends. The purpose of the game was to keep the ball in play—one team passing the ball over the colored line to the players in the opposite end of the ball ground, and vice versa, without allowing it to rebound more than once.

The team that won in a skirmish of this kind, received one point. Another means of gaining a point was to throw the ball against or over the opponent's wall, and apparently the wide ends also had to be protected, for, if the ball was driven into these courts, the team placing it there made a score.

Failure of the ball to cross the line caused a fault. The player who was unfortunate in touching the ball with a hand, foot, or some other forbidden action of his body, lost a point for his side. The game was continued until one side obtained a set number of points.

The ball player that succeeded in passing the ball through the small hole of the ring in one wall (the team's goal called tlachtemalacatl), brought the game to an immediate close with victory for his party—regardless of the point score up to the minute. A perfect shot was a rare occurrence because of the small size of the hole in the ring, and because of the rules which prevented touching the ball with hands and feet—leaving only the elbows, knees and thighs with which the master stroke could be accomplished.

First-rate players enjoyed a reputation to an extent equal to that of any renowned athlete of our day, and in token of its being an extraordinary success which rarely happened, he who won the game striking the ball through the goal had thereby a right to the cloaks of all the on-lookers, by ancient custom, law, and tradition.

The popularity of the game of tlachtli among the ancient Aztecs and neighboring tribes, and the frequency with which it was played, may be measured by the astonishing number of balls, 160,000 or more, which were extracted by the Aztecs each year as part of tribute from Tochtepec, Otatitlan, and other locales.

Turning to the actual training of the Aztecs in military tactics, we find that during each festival month, at scheduled times, the warriors and chiefs would make their appearance at the square in full regalia, and would engage in a mock skirmish and drill to gain proficiency in handling their weaponry. The presence of the youth of the Telpuchcalli was demanded so that they might observe and learn.

The students of the Telpuchcalli had already had their own sham fights within the college, to learn how to wield the heavy macana (spear), and to brandish the bow and discharge arrows; in the beginning against lifeless objects and then later against animals.

They also had to become proficient with the javelin, the dart, and sometimes with three-pointed branches so as to cause several wounds at once. The atlatl was the instrument by which they sped the darts at their targets.

Bows and arrows were found to be the most convenient for opening the combat before they came to close quarters and grappled with each other. Slings for the throwing of pebbles and stones were also among their equipment. The best weapons for close-in fighting were the sword and club, occasionally the spear.

The sword most often used was three and a half to four feet long, and four to five inches wide. It had a wooden handle, and along the entire length of the weapon, which was usually double-edged, were inserted slivers of obsidian, to maximize injury. At the beginning of an engagement, the weapon was much feared.

Defensive arms included a wooden helmet and a shield or chimalli, which was worn by the warrior on his left arm, and was made of canes netted together and interwoven with cotton two-fold, covered on the outside with gilded boards and feathers, and so strong that only a hard cross-bow shot could alone penetrate them. Blows in close combat and arrows and darts coming at full speed were warded off with this shield.

A typical battle usually opened with the warriors hurling stones by slings. Thereafter they resorted to sword and shield, the archers going in at the same time well-protected. The archers from Tehuacan sometimes were so dexterous that they sped two or three arrows at once with the same precision as one bowman would shoot alone.

After the vanguard had spent a good deal of their ammunition, they charged with sword and dart. The sword was often tied to the wrist in order that they might seize an enemy (their main object was to capture men alive), without losing their weapon. They had no style of fencing; neither did they charge directly, but skirmished back and forth.

At first, one party would turn to flee, as it seemed, the other pursuing, wounding, killing if necessary, and capturing all those that lagged in the rear. Then the party fleeing would suddenly turn back upon the pursuers, who fled in turn.

Thus they proceeded as in a tournament, until they were tired, when fresh bodies moved up to take up the fight.

The tribal war-lord retained a standing army of about two thousand within his palace grounds, carefully selected for bravery, who kept watch for his safety, and accompanied him as part of his retinue. If an outbreak or insurrection started in the city or neighboring territory, they were the ones who would rush forth in the necessary numbers to quell the outburst.

If a war was proclaimed, and more soldiers required, a general gathering of the troops within the city would follow for a quick assembling of the forces of the whole tribe. Every man, in time of war, could be called upon to serve, with the exception of children, the elderly, the weak or disabled, and in some cases, priests. In extreme instances it was commanded that no youth over fifteen years of age could remain at home.

The Conquistadors reported that at the darkest hour of the conquest, even the women fought, and that children as well as the disabled furnished their warriors with projectiles and arrows.

Each calpulli yielded a force of able-bodied men which carried on as a unit of the Aztec army, including those members of the tribe whose military pursuits were subordinated to those of their daily occupations.

The calpulli divisions formed ranks around their chiefs, and practically at the same moment, with a given signal, all moved together to procure their weapons from the public storehouses, armories and arsenals, which were usually attached to the temples of each calpulli. The stewards were already awaiting them to distribute the arms. Shortly thereafter, they offered sacrifices to the god of war, then having been blessed, could set out for war.

Consequently, in a very short time, their largest units could be mobilized, fully armed, ranked and graded under their respective leaders, ready to march forth along the causeways to the mainland, or to go by way of canoes across the lake, at a sign from their war-lord. Usually however, rehearsals were held first at each of the four quarters of their territory.

The most practical teacher in the art of war, however, is war itself. When the mournful sounds of the huehuetl drum on the main temple were heard summoning everybody to battle, not only did all the warriors gather around the chiefs, but the pupils of every Telpuchcalli who were of age hastened to join them.

At first, they acted s bearers, carrying the weapons and baggage of the warriors, but later, they entered into combat as recruits. Sometimes their campaigning apprenticeship came early, when suddenly thrust into full battle, as during the warlord Tizoc's expeditions of conquest before he assumed the chieftainship in 1481.

The people of Metzitlan, with the aid of their Huastec allies, resisted the invasion of the Aztecs with such success that Tizoc was obliged to bring into action a squadron of youths aged eighteen to twenty, in order to offset the loss of about three hundred of his more seasoned soldiers.

In another incident, this time in the early history of the rise of the Aztecs to military power, the Aztec war chief Tlacaellel, disdaining to lead his army against a neighboring city within the lake area, went into the temple schools and drew out those youths from ten to eighteen years of age whom he considered fit and who knew how to maneuver their boats and canoes. He taught them certain tactics, then led them against Cuitlahuac, and successfully stormed the city.

The youths obtained much treasure and many captives for sacrifice, for the King of Cuitlhuac reasoned that if his people could be conquered by a handful of boys, it would be foolhardy to wait for the main Aztec army to strike, for then they would be most assuredly wiped off the face of the earth.

It was in the actual fighting that the real training began, with the youths learning how to endure hunger, thirst, sun sickness, and fatigue during the long marches, cold, moisture and rain without shelter during dark nights, being obliged to sleep amid swamps, etc. They were also taught to lay in wait, ambush, set artful traps, and to follow cunningly an enemy without being seen.

But the principle teaching was on the pitched field of death when the soldiers grouped together following their chiefs, when the savage war cry was shouted, when the air was cut by the harsh buzz of the warrior shells and the Tlactecuhtli's gold drum gave orders with a quick double-beat.

The principle teaching was taking place by firing the opening salvo of arrows, by flinging thick hails of stones with their flexible slings; by seeing enemies fall at a distance and comrades drop down nearby, and they continued learning still more at the moment when the armies came into contact, pressed one another, and mingled into horrible contractions.

As we've mentioned before, the aim of the regular Aztec soldier was not to destroy the enemy immediately, but to gather them as victims for the sacrificial altars. This feat of taking a prisoner had the same import among the ancient Aztecs as the collecting of scalps among the North American Indians, but social and political recognition were the rewards held out to the Mexican warrior who brought forward a war captive and offered him for sacrifice.

It was this fact that was impressed upon the students in the Telpuchcalli as worthy of their ambitions and for which to strive, for the achievement of taking a prisoner meant for the recruits the attainment of rank of warrior.

In addition to becoming a warrior, there were placed before them other incentives for the committing of acts of bravery and daring, such as promotion, rewards, and the privilege of entrance into the warrior's paradise if death should come their way.

During the fourth month, a celebration of the feast of the god of the grain fields, Tzintantli, and of the goddess of sustenance, chicomecoatl, was held. Ears of corn put aside for sowing were carried on the backs of young virgin girls, wrapped in blankets, never more than seven ears in each bundle, and on each ear they sprinkled a few drops of "ulli" oil, then wrapped them in paper.

The arms and legs of the young girls were covered with red feathers, and on their faces they put melted tar, called Chapopoctil, sprinkled with white pyrite powder. As they went along the road, no one dared speak to them, for fear of offending the gods. After the ears of corn had been carried to the select holy place, or Cu, for blessing, they returned them again to their homes and put them at the very bottom of a trough. When sowing time came, they used them as the first seeds for the planting.

The son of a noble obtained his earlier education in the Calmecac, and began to receive instruction in the art of war at the age of fifteen, as noted in an earlier chapter. When he reached twenty, he was sent to take part in a campaign.

Prior to his departure, the father and his relatives, in keeping with the Aztec trait of ceremoniousness, invited the captains and older soldiers of this son's group to a banquet, where, after bestowing gifts upon the latter, they begged them to take good care of the young man during the war, by teaching him, how to fight and by protecting him against the enemy.

As soon as the warlike activities got under way, the warriors took the son along with them, and taught him everything necessary both for his defense and for marching on the offensive. When the battle began, they did not lose him from sight, and they brought his attention to those who were capturing an enemy so that he might learn to do the same and might have the merit of taking some captives in his first war thanks to the protection of those who had taken charge of him.

If on the battlefield the training was greater in degree of intensity, it was not, however, terminated there, for the education of both Telpuchcalli and Calmecac students proceeded anew when triumphal honors were bestowed in the capital, where the most courageous and successful recruits and warriors received their rewards.

There were set rules regarding the making of awards and honors for service in war. Success in the number of captives taken for sacrifice determined promotion, not only in the army, but also for officers of state. If those who had already taken captives took still more in later battles, they were greatly esteemed by the king, who bestowed upon them the notable honor of raising them to the rank of pilli, giving them names of braves.

They were, from that time on, eligible for election as a lord, and they could thereafter sit near the kings and eat with them. They received the insignia of brave men, such as precious stones of different colors for the lips, tassels to put on their heads, trimmed with gold and feathers.

The king also gave them beautiful and richly embroidered belts of royal lineage, and other distinctive tokens they could use all their lives. On the other hand, the young man who went to war two or three times and came back without having captured anyone either alone or with others, was called disgraceful.

Whoever reduced to captivity five or more of the enemy was placed in the rank of the greatest and most honored captains and intrepid chiefs, who were called quauhyacatl, which means "eagle who guides." To that person, the king gave a long green chin piece, and other distinctive medallions, as a sign of greatest respect.

Men, however young in years, who had successfully endured great trials in battle, deserved to be looked upon thereafter as persons of uncommon fortitude. Hence, they were particularly fitted for responsible offices of any kind. They were looked upon with deference, their voice was heard and listened to. But no privilege with their dignity was attached, except that of wearing certain distinctive ornaments; moreover, none was transmitted through them to their descendants.

The military code of the Aztecs taught to the recruit was characterized by the same severity as their other laws. Death was the penalty for failure on the part of the soldier to carry out orders, for leaving his post or colors, for falling upon the enemy before the sign was given, for appropriating plunder or prisoners from another, for assuming the badge of a higher rank, and for the freeing of a prisoner instead of holding him for sacrifice.

In many respects, the Aztecs were more progressive than the Old World in the humane aspects of war, by erecting hospitals in their principle towns for the care of the sick and wounded, and also as a permanent asylum for the disabled soldier.

These were placed under the supervision of surgeons, who, it can be said, were so far better than those in Europe that they did not protract the cure in order to increase their pay. In fact, among other things worthy of note with the highest of praise, Montezuma allotted the city of Colhuacan as a hospital for all invalids who after having done faithful service to the crown, either in military or civil employments, required a provision for their age or infirmities.

There was a hospital at Tezcuco for all those who had lost their eyesight in war, or who had become from any other cause unfit for service, where they were supported at royal expense according to their stations, and frequently visited by the king himself.

The student of good breeding would accept the customs of the Telpuchcalli and never leave of his own volition, even if he had become of age; only upon the request of the chief would he make his departure.

Graduation from the Telpuchcalli took place when the young student was granted the rank of warrior. As soon as he had distinguished himself admirably on the battlefield, he was accepted into the ranks of adult society, and at liberty to take a wife.

The parents in most cases retained the right to arrange marriages, and as a result, there was little actual "wooing" among the ancient Mexicans. Among the masses, before a young man could look forward to matrimony, it was first determined whether he had the capacity to earn his living.

With respect to the prospective bride, the ability to cook and weave was regarded as being of greater concern than beauty. Sometimes the young man would make known to his parents the girl whom he desired to wed. The age at which the male youths usually married was from twenty to twenty-two; the females from fifteen to eighteen years.

The ancient Aztecs deemed marriage indispensable for the conservation and increase of the race, and as a result, all those youths who refused to wed were looked upon with disfavor and subsequently expelled from the tribe. Only those were excused who were naturally helpless and made vows of permanent chastity. All women, too, were duty bound to marry, with the exception of those who took vows for the temple service, were physically deformed, or in other ways looked upon as abandoned.

When the choice of a suitable wife was decided upon, the parents consulted the astrologers, who, after considering the birthday of the youths, decided on the happiness or unhappiness of the match. If, from the combination of the signs attending their births, they pronounced the alliance unpropitious, that young maid was abandoned for the purpose of the union, and another was sought.

If on the contrary, they predicted happiness for the couple, the young girl was demanded of her parents by certain women amongst them called Cihuatlanque, or solicitors, who were the most elderly and respectable among the kindred of the youth.

These women went the first time at midnight to the house of the prospective bride, carrying a present for the parents. Here they demanded her of them in a humble and respectful style. The first demand was, according to the custom of the nation, always refused, however advantageous and eligible the marriage might appear to the parents, who gave some plausible reasons for their refusal.

After a few days passed, the solicitors returned to repeat their demand, using prayers and arguments also, in order to obtain their request, giving an account of the rank and fortune of the youth, and of what he would make the dowry of his wife, and also gaining information of that which she could bring to the match on her part.

The parents replied to this second request, that it was necessary to consult their relations and connections, and to find out the inclinations of their daughter, before they could come to any resolution.

The female solicitors returned no more; as the parents themselves conveyed, by means of other women of their kindred, a decisive answer to the request. A favorable answer being at last obtained, and a day appointed for the nuptials, the parents, after exhorting their daughter to fidelity and obedience to her husband, and to such conduct in life as would do honor to her family, conducted her with a numerous company and music, to the house of her prospective father-in-law; if of noble birth, she was carried in a litter. The bridegroom and the prospective father and mother-in-law received her at the gate of the house, with four women.

At meeting, the bride and bridegroom reciprocally offered incense to one another; then the bridegroom, taking the bride by the hand, let her into the hall or chamber which was prepared for the nuptials. They both sat down upon a newly woven mat spread in the middle of the chamber, and close to the fire.

Then a priest tied a point of the huipilli or wedding gown of the bride with the tilmatli, or mantle of the bridegroom, and in this ceremony, often officiated by several priests, the matrimonial contract chiefly consisted.

The wife now made some turns around the fire, and then returning to her mat, she along with her husband, offered incense to their gods, and exchanged presents with each other. A sumptuous repast followed next. The married pair sat upon the mat, giving mouthfuls to each other alternately, and to the guests in their places.

The newly married couple then passed the next four days in prayer and fasting, fearing that otherwise the punishment of heaven would fall upon them. The priests in attendance were the persons who adjusted their bed to sanctify their marriage.

It was not until the fourth night that the marriage was consummated.

7

Arts and Sciences of the Aztecs

Innumerable studies attesting to the cultural and scientific accomplishments of the ancient Aztecs before the coming of the Spaniards, (not to mention those of a deprecatory nature) have been made; therefore, for the purposes of this book, only a brief examination of some of their arts and sciences will be made.

Religious and military instruction, ceremonial and the education of the will were not all the Aztecs desired to attain; their training also encompassed cultural and scientific learning. We know that the higher priesthood representing the learned class taught hieroglyphic reading and writing, oratory, arithmetic, the calendar, divination, astronomy and astrology, medicine, history, geography, poetry, songs and hymns for the gods, dancing, music, mythology, law and tradition. How they graded the work of the special subjects, and the extent to which their knowledge was empirical, is difficult to ascertain from the historical sources we have at hand to date.

Even though the Aztecs were enlightened in all the different kinds of hieroglyphic painting, in the main, they made most of the method of direct representation, employing a pictographic and partially hieroglyphical form of writing. These were practically limited to place names, personal names, month and day names, numbers and principle objects of commerce.

There were no word pictures for adverbs, adjectives or conjunctions, and no representation of abstract ideas. Such hieroglyphs for example as the Chinese symbol for "danger" which represents a child standing on the edge of a cliff, were unknown to the Aztecs. Further, some of the Aztec signs were in no way realistic, and had a definite meaning by common consent alone. Others were abbreviated and conventionalized pictures of objects. Thus the head of a god or an animal frequently appeared as the sign of the whole.

The most important and interesting word signs were so-called rebuses, in which separate syllables or groups of syllables were represented by more or less conventionalized pictures. The whole word picture was then made up of syllable pictures which indicated phonetically the word as a whole. Color and position also played a part in the hieroglyph. A particular emphasis was placed upon the dress, ornaments and face painting of the individual, since they indicated, among other things, rank.

As awkward as the Aztec picture-writing was, however, it appears to have served the needs of the nation quite well. With the aid of their hieroglyphics, all of their laws, civil and criminal, court records, rules for domestic economy, taxes, their tribute rolls indicating the levies to be exacted from specific towns, geographical and topographical plans and the charts of rivers and cities, land titles, mechanical employments, their ceremonies and different phases of their ancient religion, their calendars, both sacred and secular, astronomical calculations, their methods of divination, mythology, portraits, images of the gods, kings, heroes, animals and plants were all set upon records.

The class of artists whose business it was to carry out this particular kind of work of telling a particular story, or imparting a definite message, or depicting a special set of relations, did so by the combined resources of representation and symbolism, as we have already noted, and it would appear that, in general, no unnecessary details made their appearance in their work. If however, the painter's decorative instincts led him to embellish his pages, such embellishment was always a part of the general design, and directly related to the current themes.

These artists, who often were skillful artisans, worked according to strict rules. Their figures of men and beasts, though often expressive in attitude, were generally stiff and conventional. The rigidity of fixed standards was a hallmark of their trade.

The ancient Aztecs had a complex calendar system, and with this, and their picture-writing, they were also enabled to record their political annals which went back to a period long before the founding of Tenochtitlan.

These included accounts of migrations, the succession of rulers, their many campaigns, the genealogies of varies nobles, and events of fundamental importance such as the details surrounding the election of tribal chieftains, the successful erection of public structures, the planning of public ventures, the distribution of conquered lands to warriors and nobles, the reforms and other changes effectuated by various rulers in the management of tribal affairs.

While an accurate chronology was out of the question for all of their historical events, a good approximation was quite possible, and the Aztecs were able to point out with exactitude of many of the most important happenings in their more recent history, the time being written on the margin, alongside of the particular event being depicted.

We can classify these types of records in the following way: ancient history (ueue tlatolli): contemporary history (quin axcan tlatolli); and year counts. Those year counts on paper were called xiuhtlapohualamatl, and those painted were called xiuhtlacuilolli. Annual accounts, year by year. Those on paper were called cexiuhamatl, and those that were painted were called cexiuhtlacuilolli.

A specific painting of each year was called cecemilhuitlacuilolli. A book of each day was called cecemilhuiamoxtle. A count, recorded day by day was called cemilhuitonalpohualli.

There was an amazing variety of types of histories and the issues contained therein. Only a fairly large number of specially trained men could possibly have created them, and indeed the Nahuan records frequently speak of a guild of artisan-writers.

For the purpose of evaluating justly the historical picture-writing of the Aztecs, it must be viewed in conjunction with the oral tradition to which it was allied. It cannot be expressed too strongly the care which parents and masters took to instruct their children and pupils in the history of the nation. They made them learn speeches and discourses which they could not express by drawing; they put the events of their ancestors into verse and taught them to sing-speak them.

This tradition dispelled their doubts and undid the ambiguity which paintings alone might have occasioned, and by the assistance of these monuments perpetrated the memory of their heroes, and of virtuous examples, their mythology, their writers, their laws, and their customs.

It is certain then, that their hieroglyphics ought not to be regarded as a complete history, but more in the nature of monuments of tradition, mnemonic devices, or memory aids.

Complete narrations were most likely associated with each historical painting, and the narrator, by scanning the text occasionally, could maintain the continuity of events he was relating.

Among primitive peoples, exceptionally tenacious memories are developed which cannot be duplicated in a modern civilization, since we rely upon the written word and our various media to strengthen our memories. Undoubtedly the ancient Mexicans possessed like retentive powers, and the purpose of the codices was to forestall possible errors from creeping in.

This last was impossible, however, under the circumstances because even if the specially selected and trained narrators passed on the information to similarly carefully selected and trained men, there were numerous dangers which could increase the chances of error.

Agave paper and animal skins on which they did their painting and recording do not last forever; some paintings with the passing of the years become illegible, while others are destroyed either by accident or willfully, while still others are lost. Finally, interpretations will vary in succeeding generations as viewpoints of those periods changed.

It is not without irony that contemporary sources always seem to retain their value, but general histories seem to be always written from particular viewpoints that are bound to be reinterpreted and misinterpreted. Certain exaggerations inevitably take place, simply because the historians of each particular ruler interpret past events in terms of that particular ruler's reign.

In the schools of the priests where the youth were instructed in the various arts and sciences, those who were to pursue the vocation of hieroglyphic painting were taught the manipulation of the characters assigned to each of their particular subjects. In a historical project, for example, one student would be responsible for the chronology, while another looked after the events.

The various aspects of their work were thus apportioned automatically. The students, enlightened in all that was previously known in their several fields of knowledge, were trained to enlarge still further the bounds of their far from perfect science.

The picture writings were used as a kind of stenography, an aggregate of notes indicating to the proficient much more than could be ordinarily imparted by a literal translation.

This union of the written word and the oral embodied what must be considered the literature of the Aztecs. There were at least five major themes throughout these books written with figures and characters. The first dealt with years and periods, and was historical in nature.

The second dealt with all the festivals that took place year-round. The third dealt with dreams and the omens which they foretold. The forth dealt with baptism, and the names they gave to their children. The fifth dealt with the various rites, and prognostications which they used at marriages and other complex ceremonies.

Though the Aztecs were barbarians and without letters, they were exceedingly orderly in counting time. They likewise painted the achievements of war, and the success of the principle lords, the tempests and heavenly signs, the various pestilences and famines, noting the time of reign in which they occurred, and all the lords who reigned up to the arrival of the Spaniards. They called this book "the computation of the years."

These hieroglyphic texts, each a collection of pictures making up the topic of an individual study, consisted of a single long leaf, with an average width of six or seven inches, and in some cases were over thirty feet in length. This single sheet was sometimes done up into a roll, but most often pressed into volumes, in screen fashion, so that when it was opened, the leaves revealed themselves to the eye.

Tablets of wood, handsomely carved and painted, were placed as covers at each end to protect the contents. Some of the most interestingly embellished book covers made use of a turquoise-mosaic design material on fine, brilliantly lacquered wood.

The hieroglyphics were painted on both sides of the leaf which was made at different times of cotton cloth, or skins carefully prepared with a compound of silk and gum; but most frequently of an excellent fabric of vegetable origin from the macerated leaves of the aloe, the Mexican maguey plant, which grows abundantly over the Mexican plateaus.

After the surface of the paper, resembling somewhat the Egyptian papyrus was glazed with a very thin covering of lime, and polished to receive the text, the pictographs and hieroglyphics were painted on with a brush in brilliant colors which included white obtained from chalk, red from cochineal, two yellows, vegetable and mineral, blue from certain flowers, and black from the coal soot of the coatl palm.

The mixing of colors was known, and brilliant greens, purples and browns are also to be found. The prime colors were often present in more than one shade, while all colors were bordered with black.

Reading of the manuscripts was from left to right, as we do, across the folds of the page, both back and front being used. As it was possible to peruse and refer to each page distinctly, this arrangement had evident benefits over the rolls of the ancient Egyptians.

Since the Aztecs were in possession of books, the inference that a portion of their teaching must have come directly from the texts by having the students in the schools learn and interpret the picture hieroglyphics would perhaps be acceptable.

The number of persons, however, outside of the more erudite, the historians and lawyers, learned priests and advanced students, etc., who were proficient in the interpretation of the codices, was in all probability quite small.

The art of oratory occupied the attention and efforts of the ancient Aztecs to a great extent, notwithstanding the fact that they were very far from being acquainted with all its virtues. The Aztecs were a very ceremonious people, and, as we have already seen, seized upon any meeting or occasion of some importance to deliver long eloquent speeches.

Children were taught the importance of speaking well at an early age, and those who were fore-ordained to be orators, were taught from their infancy to speak properly, and memorize the most renowned discourses of their forefathers that had been handed down through the generations. Their eloquence was employed in councils, and devoted often to delivering addresses to the new tribal chieftains, in judicious and elegant expressions of congratulation.

The fact that the ancient Aztecs were ardent lovers of singing, music, and dancing, and that they devoted much time to them, is often mentioned by the early historians. These arts are constantly represented as eminent features of their civilization, and without them no state or community function of real social importance, in government, religion and war was complete.

They were requisite to the divine services held in the teocallis and the receptions and banquets, large or small, gained their principle charm and splendor from their relationships with these arts.

It had been the practice, before the coming of Cortes, for every community, every chief, and every person of consequence, to maintain a troupe of singers and dancers, compensating them regularly.

The patrons of these artists took an intense personal concern in their preparation, and were very impatient with carelessness in the performance of duties; if the occasion was of great importance, and any of the singers touched upon a false note, or a drummer missed time, or a dancer assumed an improper pose one too many times, that unlucky performer was immediately demanded to come forward, placed in bonds, and without delay taken away to receive serious punishment.

With such exacting judges to please, it is easily understood why it was necessary to start the training at an early age, and to establish definite places for instruction with qualified teachers. It was one of the distinct duties of the teachers of the Calmecac to teach carefully the traditions of the country as embodied in the verses of the sacred songs and hymns which were written in characters in their books.

The Aztecs, however, like most American Indians, were not a musical people as measured by modern European and American standards, being imperfect in the respect that while musical instruments were used in most of their religious functions, and all dances, the range of these was limited.

Of those musical instruments known to us, there are two dissimilar kinds of drums; four-fingered flutes of bamboo and pottery, smaller whistles with two-fingered holes; no string instruments, with the exception of a musical bow; the cara-paces of turtles beat with antler; conch shells with the ends cut off used as trumpets; jingling of strings of small univalve shells producing pleasant sounds; whistling jars, and several other types of nondescript percussion paraphernalia.

The huehuetl, a vertical drum, was a cylinder of wood, hollowed out of a log, usually at least three feet in height and thicker than a man's body. Magnificently carved, it was also painted on the outside with animal figures, gods, and religious scenes. The upper end was covered with the skin of a deer, well-dressed and stretched, which at the proper moment could be tightened and slackened, to cause its sound to become sharper or deeper.

It was played by beating with the fingers or knuckles only, upon the parch-ment, but a great deal of adroitness and skill were essential. It was said that it pro-duced a sound so ominous that it could be heard at a distance of two leagues.

The teponaztli, a cylindrical, horizontal wooden drum, was made out of a hol-lowed out log bearing two lateral slits in the center. It was played with two drum-sticks, their ends covered with ulli or rubber. Their sizes ranged from very small ones that could be worn about the neck, to large ones approaching five feet in length which could be heard at a distance of two or three miles. The war captains used them on the battlefield to rally the troops and discourage the enemy.

The tecomapiloa, or suspended vase, was considered superior to the teponaz-tli, was made from a solid block of wood, with a jutting ridge on its upper sur-face, and another opposite, on its bottom. From this, one or more gourds or vases were suspended, which increased or softened the sound when the upper ridge was struck with the ulli sticks.

The omichicahuaztli, a rather curious musical instrument, consisted of a long bone, human or animal, or a horn deeply notched by a series of grooves or trans-verse cuts on one side. The player would hold it in his left hand, and scratch across it with a conch shell, producing a mournful sound.

One of its signature uses was to give time to dancers. The original form of the omichicahuaztli consisted of the bones of the dead, and its prime function was to serve as a musical instrument in funeral ceremonies of the kings and great war-riors.

The tetzilacatl, or sheet gong, was a broad piece of thin copper hanging from a cord, which was played by striking it with sticks or the hand. The use of this par-ticular instrument was restricted chiefly to the sacred music in the temples. The musicians who played the sacred music were members of the priesthood.

The ayacachtli consisted of a deep earthenware jar or dried gourd within which there were pebbles attached to a handle. This rattle had as its function the marking of time in various songs and dances. An elaboration of this was the aya-cachicahualitztli, or the "arrangement of rattles." This was a long thin board, about six feet long, to which there were attached copper bells, rattles, and cylindrical pieces of hardened wood. Shaking this produced jingle jangles agreeable to the ear.

There were also included among their musical instruments varied forms of flutes of bamboo, bone, or pottery. Often, these were carved with human heads, and were regarded as important instruments, since the leader of the choir of singers in the temple, known as tlapizacatzin, or "noble flute player," used them regularly.

Large conch shells from the seashores were converted into wind instruments or trumpets called quiquiztli, and the hoarse notes which came forth from them carried great distances. Still another of their instruments was the suspended dried shell of the tortoise, which was struck to produce its solemn sound.

The Aztecs understood and applied the natural phenomenon of harmonies. For this understanding, the use of sea shells was of prime importance. The antiquity of the use of the shell is not easy to determine, but it seems likely that it long antedated the Aztecs. The shells of Teotihuacan tend to prove that peoples at least as early as the Toltecs made use of it.

The marine snail-shell provided a long tube serving the same purpose as ancient oriental cultures were served by the animal horn. In playing them, which the Indians did for thousands of years, they received a music lesson from nature.

Some of these shells, preserved to this day in the National Museum of Mexico, are capable of producing natural harmonic scales that can be sounded with great ease.

With this instrument, the Aztecs discovered a series of natural scales that obey a series of acoustic laws which are the basis of the musical system of the occident. They based on these scales the foundation of a musical system using octaves, fifths, and thirds, and applying this knowledge, obtained their pentatonic scale without semitones.

They learned these lessons well, and put them into practice consistently; not one of the Aztec instruments produces sounds outside this system. For example, the teponaxtle is a cylindrical piece of wood, hollowed out to produce a sound box. Two wooden tongues, parts of the same cylinder, produce two different notes.

Various of these that exist to this day produce the following musical intervals: fifth, fourth, major third, minor third, and major second. All of their other instruments used the pentatonic scale.

How did the music produced on these instruments sound when played together? What forms did their music take? What sentiments did their music express? These questions can be answered if we think of the various religious or military contexts and occasions they occurred in, and if we understand the poetry to which it was allied.

As to its form, we will probably never arrive at a definite, unchallengeable understanding of that, for this is a question of general feeling, of penetrating the totality of Indian culture. Some light is thrown on it, however, by the pure indigenous traditional music still heard in various remote locations in Mexico.

In any case, the objective and incontrovertible data of the instruments themselves are of fundamental importance.

It will be understood that a musical tradition so strong, so complete, so firmly rooted, could not be overthrown or supplanted. The Conquistadors did not even try to combat it. From the beginning, they accepted the continuation of the pagan rites, merely adapting them to Christianity.

For this reason, it is still possible, in the atria of many churches in small towns, and in the great religious processions of today to hear the Indians playing their huehuetl, the teponaxtle, and their small flutes, unadulterated reminiscences of pre-conquest music. Nor could the Conquistadors have battled against the custom of singing the Aztec traditional hymns.

Much attention was also given to teaching the young people the manner of dancing. This was an important feature of their education, for as they learned the dances, they were procuring a clear conception of tribal tradition and lineage. Dancing played an important role in the religious and military life of the Aztecs.

There were a vast number of dances, given names based on the name of the dance or the circumstances of the particular festival for which it was called. The dances were nearly always arranged with singing that was conformable to the beating of the drums and the other instruments.

Dances brought to an end virtually every festival of importance, not infrequently carrying over to several nights, since most of the dancing occurred at night. The two sexes were segregated for the most part, the most prominent exception being the dance offered in homage to the war-lord huitzilopochtli, in which the men, dancing together with the women, placed their arms around the latter's shoulders or necks.

At noon of the feast-day of Huitzilopochtli, a magnificent dance began in the temple, led by the most valiant warriors. Some of these groups were called Otomi, others Ququachicti, these two groups leading the dance. Immediately following came others called Tequicacque, and after these came the Telpuchiaque, then the Tiachoaoan, and finally the young men known as the Telpupu-chti.

There were also women taking part in this dance, prostitutes among them, dancing either one woman between two men, or one man between two women, all three holding hands.

The most sacred of all the dances was performed at the festival of the god of fire, which was enacted by the priests alone, who covered themselves with black paint to symbolize darkness and light. They carried two torches in each hand, and gathered in a circle in a sitting position, then slowly moved around the "divine brazier," until at the end of the dance, they cast their torches into it.

No doubt, this most ancient of sacred dances must have been impressive to those who witnessed it at nighttime from the base of the pyramid and heard the distant solemn chanting of the dancers. To watchers from afar, the fire and the lighted torches revolving around must have seemed like a great central star with its burning satellites circling about it.

The Aztec dances and concerts were nearly always held in the open air, and depending on the nature of the occasion, in the temples, village squares, and courtyards of individual homes. Many started in the morning hours and lasted until evening, sometimes carrying on far into the night. The musicians would gather in the center of the square, with the professional singers standing or sitting around them.

Upon a given signal, the two best-trained singers would open the ceremony by pronouncing the first syllables of the song in a slow manner, but with decided force, then the drums would join in with a low tone which increased, gradually, by degrees, as the song went along.

The other singers soon added their voices until the whole chorus was partici-pating, and finally, when the surrounding onlookers recognized the words of some familiar song, they would unite their voices with those of the chorus, mea-suring time by unison movements of their hands and feet.

Each verse of the song was sung over as many as three or four times before going on to the next, and it was also their custom to choose for the first hours of the festival those songs which were of the slowest measure and least emotional in character.

The songs, even with the repetitions, seldom continued over an hour each. To this day, the old love of song and dance persists in the Indian villages, and though the themes may be different, the outward form has retained many of the ancient characteristics.

The most professional Aztec singers had to have a clear mind and strong memory. He or she would have had to compose songs himself, and learn those of others, and always be ready to impart both of these to others of his craft. He sang with a well-trained voice, and was careful to practice in private before appearing before the public. On the other hand, the unworthy singer could be counted on to be ignorant and indolent, at once envious and boastful.

The Aztec singing voice has been described by the early historians as harsh, strident, and disagreeable to European ears, largely occupying the contra-bass ranges; persons fortunate in possessing such a voice cultivated it diligently, and often enjoyed great popularity.

The songs of the Aztecs varied with the months and seasons, and were of many kinds. They dealt with historical themes, such as mythical legends of a heroic age, warlike feats of their own time, and like ourselves, some treated of love and pleasure.

Others were of hunting and games, odes, often didactic in nature, offering some moral or lesson, valuable for the development of proper habits of life; still others were composed for the gods, many of which raised high their praises in order to receive from them desired favors. Some were straight and true songs, songs of the noble springtime, flower songs, songs of destitution and compassion, geographical songs, and others songs of lamentation for the dead.

These ancient Aztec songs revealed a high standard of poetic imagery. They often did not rhyme per-se, but instead exhibited much rhythm. They did not divide their lyrics and poems into lines, as is done in modern poetry and song, for as they were made to be sung and danced to as well as occasionally recited, the music ran uninterruptedly without a break, until the end of the paragraph.

Other songs and poems abound in archaic forms and endings, expressed in language containing so many symbolical religious allusions that they are difficult to explain because they mystify historical facts with obscure metaphors that scarcely anyone can understand unless special attention is given to their construction.

The most renowned Aztec poet was Nezahualcoyotl, of the royal house of Tezcuco. He ruled over Tezcuco from 1431 to 1472, and passed away at the old age of eighty years, in 1472. Several verses from one of his famous poems on the inconstancy of life and the certainty of death are worthy of repeating here. They have been translated as follows:

"All the earth is a grave, and naught escapes it; nothing is so perfect that it does not fall and disappear. The rivers, brooks, fountains and waters flow on, and never return to their joyous beginnings; they hasten on to the vast realms of Tlaloc. That which was yesterday is not today; and let not that which is today trust to live tomorrow.

"The caverns of earth are filled with pestilential dust which once was the bones, the flesh, the bodies of great ones who sat upon thrones; deciding causes, ruling assemblies, governing armies, conquering provinces, possessing with pride, majesty, fortune, praise and dominion. These glories have passed like the dark smoke thrown out by the fires of Popocatepetl, leaving no monuments but the rude skins on which they are written."

Another poem, which the native historian Ixtlilxochitl attributed to Nezahualcoyotl, and translated into Castilian, expresses and Epicurean philosophy, that is, to seek relief from the anxieties of the future in the delights and pleasures of the present.

"Banish care," the poem begins: "If there are bounds to pleasure, the saddest life must also have and end. Then weave the chaplet of flowers and sing thy songs in praise of all-powerful God; for the glory of this world soon fades away.

"Rejoice in the green freshness of spring; for the day will come when you shall sigh for these joys in vain, when the scepter will pass from your hands, your servants will wander desolate in your courts, your sons and the sons of your nobles will drink the dregs of distress, and all the pomp of your victories and triumphs shall live only in their recollection.

"Yet the remembrance of the just shall not pass away from the nations, and the good you have done shall ever be held in honor. The goods of this life, its glories and its riches are but lent to us, its substance but an illusory shadow, and the things of today will surely change on the coming of the morrow. Then gather the fairest flowers from your gardens to bind around your brow, and seize the joys of the present before they perish."

The prayer of an Aztec chieftain upon his election is also worthy of being repeated here:

"Grant me Lord a little light; be it no more than a glow-worm gives which goes about by night, to guide me through this life, this dream that lasts but mere days wherein are many things on which to stumble, and many things on which to laugh; and others like a stony path along which one goes stumbling."

The love of nature was strongly developed among the ancient Aztecs, and is manifested in the delicate imagery of many of their poems. For example:

"Truly as I walk along I hear the rocks as they were replying to the sweet songs of the flowers, truly the glittering chattering water answers; the bird-green fountain, there it sings, to dash forth and sing again; the many sweet-singing birds scatter their songs and bless the earth pouring out their sweet voices."

The English language has taken many words from the Aztec, such as avocado, chili, chocolate, cocoa, copal, coyote, ocelot, and tomato. The Aztec is a language of the unifying type which is able to combine two or more particular words into a unified entity, so that one word may carry the meaning of a complete sentence. For instance, the name of Montezuma signifies, "when the chief is angry he shoots to heaven;" tlatocatecpanchantizinco means, "the revered house of the sovereign family."

One of the most remarkable examples of a real composition of words can be found in "amatlacuilolitcotiaxtlahuilli," which signifies "the reward given to the messenger who carries a paper on which is painted tidings." Then too, there is the word "notlazomehuiztespixcatatzin," meaning "venerable priest whom I cherish as my father," which was used by the Aztecs in addressing favorite priests.

Interesting to note, the letters b,d,f,g, and r, are not found in the Aztec language.

The Aztecs also had various theatrical displays, rooted in pantomime, in which the actors concealed their faces with masks, and dressed in costumes of multi-colored feathers, representing birds, butterflies, and animals, as well as humans.

There are accounts of festivals held for Quetzalcoatl in which there was, in the area of the temple of this god, a small theatre, perhaps thirty feet square, adorned with boughs, from which were suspended many birds and rabbits.

The actors appeared as burlesque characters, feigning deafness, sickness, blindness, and various other crippling afflictions. Those who had colds and infections were coughing and spitting, the lame halting; all recited their complaints and misfortunes, which produced infinite mirth among the audience.

By evening's end, however, Quetzalcoatl had brought relief from their pain, suffering, and afflictions, and all the spectators joined in a grand dance to bring the festival to a close.

The Aztecs possessed an extensive literature which was cast into trochaic meter, and memorized, because of their desire to preserve it as oral history, in the absence of an adequate system of writing. This ancient Mexican literature falls naturally into six classes: the sacred literature of the temples; the elaborate formulas of civic societies, the didactic literature of the schools; court poetry; family instruction; and incantations and conjurations.

The sacred literature of the Aztec temple is the most extensive. It included the vast body of ritualistic literature connected with the worship of the gods. It embraces religious ceremonies, prayers, invocations, salutations, traditional and legendary histories of a religious nature, descriptions of ceremonial vestments, symbols, signs, and attributes of the deities, to which was added whatever scientific knowledge the priests possessed.

No less interesting was the elaborate formulae of ancient Mexican civic life and society. It seemed to portray every civic activity in the later days of the Aztec empire. The addresses of the judges in their courts; ambassadors from the court of the Montezumas to tributary nations and foreign powers; all cast their salutations in verse which seems to have been ritualistic and always delivered in the same form. Marriage ceremonies and all other civic occasions had their corresponding ritualistic literature, taught in the temple schools, cast in identical form.

When an Aztec priest came to receive a newborn child into the nation, he acted according to rigorously prescribed metric formulae, as existing Aztec documents demonstrate. When a hunter went forth to hunt, custom imposed upon him a most elaborate ceremony, all of which was cast in meter. This he had to go through with great precision and according to prescribed form, in order to secure the success of his venture.

When illness or insomnia visited an Aztec Indian, the necromancer was called in to drive it away. He chanted verses centuries old, in which the gods of the sub terrestrial world, and the deities of the night, were called upon to help. These long formulae were filled with Aztec classical allusions, and words filled with various magical meaning.

Aztec Court poetry consisted of songs composed and sung at the courts of Mexico, Texcoco, Tlaxcala, Huexotzinco, and other literary centers, by the court poets, for the entertainment of the sovereigns, princes, nobles and bards.

These songs are quite distinct from the other metric literature of the ancient Mexicans. A great many of the compositions, frequently florid and imaginatively poetical, are written in a variety of meters suggestive of remarkable cultivation of verse.

Family instruction often took the form of exhortations, or Huehue Tlatalli, made to their children. With these long-form admonitions, they educated them. They were not only delivered by word of mouth, but had to be memorized, just as many Christians learn to recite their prayers and the more important parts of divine law.

The goal was that after they had been memorized, they were put into practice, and in this way they were handed down from father to son and grandson, etc., and thus never forgotten.

Conjurations constituted a literature by themselves at the time of the Conquest, which bears evidence of being much older than the temple literature, since they have to do almost completely with the older nature gods of which the chief was Ome Teotl, the Fire God. He, together with the Tlalocs or water gods, the Rain Gods, the Wind Gods, and the Night God, the Earth Mother, had been displaced as principle deities by the great state and court gods under the Aztecs, with the one exception of Quetzalcoatl, the Wind God, still worshiped by the descendants of the Toltecs.

The Aztecs were not uninformed about the rudiments of geography, for we see, as evidence of the fact, the precise uniformity of certain astronomical sculptures, symmetry in the marking out and dividing of the circle, the apportionment of lands, and the ascertaining of the dimensions of areas.

Included among their codices are several maps which performed the function of not only showing the extent and boundaries of land possessions, but also the exact locations of places, and the condition of the country: whether it was fertile or barren, or even if a state of war or peace existed. Some also indicate the direction of coasts, and the course of rivers.

One of the native maps in the Codex Mendoza reveals to us that they looked upon their capital city as a square, surrounded by water, and divided into four sections of equal size by diagonal cross-streams or canals.

In the manuscript department of the British Museum, there is to be an ancient Mexican picture-map painted in different colors on some woven material formed of two strips sewn together and measuring 180cm. by 105 cm. According to one of the interpretations, this particular map was drawn to furnish a census of the people living in a number of towns within a large area, and the relative positions of their homes and property.

Some of their codices contained maps which depicted their early migrations, and which have been pored over in an attempt to ascertain from where they originally came. The first few plates of Duran's Atlas deal with the islands and mainland from which it is believed these Indians came, and the many towns and territories through which they passed until they reached the valley of Mexico.

The places or towns in these documents are portrayed by hieroglyphs, and frequently, the character of the section of country is devoted to pictures of typical vegetation, such as maguey plants, for the highlands, and palms for the lowlands.

Maps were often made for informative purposes. For example, merchants, after completing long journeys into new territories, were able to offer much valuable information concerning enemy tribes through the use of maps. When Cortes made his appearance on the Mexican coast, Montezuma shortly afterwards received, in addition to a verbal account, paintings of the Spaniards, their horses, ships, and their later progress into the interior.

Cortes, in his first letter to Charles V, wrote that after several requests were made to learn if there was any safe harbor for vessels in the Mexican Gulf, Montezuma proffered to him a painting of the whole coast, from the port of Chalchiuhculcan (now Vera Cruz), to the river Coatzacualco.

Bernal Diaz Del Castillo, of Cortes' original party, relates that this particular painting appeared on a cloth of maguey, and all the rivers and roads along the coast were depicted clearly. He also wrote that Cortes, in a long and arduous cruise to the Bay of Honduras had recourse to a chart which had been given him by the lords of Coatzacualco, in which all the rivers and certain locations were recorded from the coast of Coatzacualco to Huejocalian.

Peter Martyr, in the fifth decade of his De Orbe Noval, specifically states, "One of the maps we have examined is thirty feet long, and not quite so wide. It is painted on white cotton cloth. All the plains and provinces, whether vassal or hostile to Montezuma, are there represented, as well as the lofty mountains which completely surround the plain.

The map also shows the southern coast ranges, whose inhabitants stated that off the coast lie the islands we have above described as producing an abundance of spices, gold, and precious stones."

While the above may prove that the Aztecs possessed a knowledge of geography, it does not give us an inkling to what extent geography, as a formal subject, was taught, and if so, how, and for whom.

In arithmetic, the Aztecs devised a quinary-vigesimal system, that is, one based primarily on twenties, and secondarily, on fives. The number five was expressed by a word meaning, "a hand taken," and the number ten by "two hands;" the word for twenty, "cempoalli," denoted a "complete count," signifying, most likely, all the fingers and toes of a person. The numbers one to twenty were represented by a similar number of dots or small circles.

Definite names were given to the first five, after which they were indicated by joining the fifth and two for seven, and so on. Separate names were also given to ten and fifteen, which could be united with the first four also, to represent a higher figure.

In their hieroglyphic writings, one was expressed by a dot, five by a bar, and twenty by a flag. Large sums were calculated by twenties, and in hieroglyphics, by merely repeating the number of flags.

Four hundred, which was the square of twenty, was depicted by either a tree or a plume, and eight thousand, the cube of twenty, was represented by an incense pouch. For instance, the number 8,888, would appear as a pouch, two plumes, four flags, a bar, and three dots.

This was the entire arithmetical system of notation of the Aztecs by the combination of which they were able to denote any quantity. For greater precision, fractions of the larger sums were indicated by painting only a part of the object. Hence, half or a quarter of a plume, or of a pouch, stood for that proportion of their respective sums, and so on.

Though their system may seem awkward to us, it should be recalled that theirs was no more so than the one pursued by the great mathematicians of antiquity, both schools being unacquainted with the method of ascertaining value, to a great extent, by the relative position on the figure.

To continue, we find that the Aztecs were completely unaware of the uses of balances, scales, or weights. Cortes records that when he passed through the great market at Tenochtitlan, he noticed that all articles were sold by number and measure. For example, when the sale of an item was consummated, it was measured by the length of a cord which could be passed around the bundle.

Whatever the lineal standard of the Aztecs may have been, it was widely recognized, very exact, and officially defined and protected. In the great market of Mexico, to which thousands flocked from the neighboring areas, there were regularly appointed government officers to examine the measures used by the merchants, and compare them with the correct standard. If they fell short, the measures were broken and the merchant severely punished as an enemy to the public weal.

On the road, the Aztecs measured distances numerically by the stops of the carriers or resting places, for instance, describing the distance between two markets or hamlets to be two or three or four resting places. Even though this method of measuring distance on the road might seem to us to be vague, to the Aztecs, actual usage had attached comparatively definite ideas of distance to these terms.

Along the highways, posts or stones were to be found with marks upon them showing how many of these neceuilli, resting places, or netlatolli, sitting places, there were to the next market-towns.

Since competition was keen among the different markets, each erected its own posts or milestones, recording its distances, and placing a curse upon all who did not attend or who were enticed by the seemingly superior attractions of its rivals.

An arrow was used by the Aztecs as a measure of length from one elbow to the tip of the hand. The Aztecs also had a standard measure of length called the octocatl which they used in marking out grounds and constructing buildings. In some of the plans of fields which have come down to us, the area is indicated by the native numerals on one side of the plan. The word meaning to survey or measure land is tlalpoa, literally "to count land," from "tlalli," or land, and "poa," to count.

Included among the sports of the ancient Aztecs were the sacred ball game tlachtli which was usually played for stakes by both participants and audience, and volador, that religious function symbolizing the passage of the year. Military fights, such as between the students of the Calmecac and Telpuchcalli, jousting competitions in shooting arrows and throwing darts for prizes; racing, wrestling, tumbling and other gymnastic contests; hunting and swimming.

In addition to the simple forms of entertainment such as riddles, and conundrums, there was a favorite game of the Aztecs in their popular amusements, called patolli. The game was played on a fine palm mat on which was painted from corner to corner, a design like a cross.

Within the hollow of the design, a series of little sections or squares were marked off by certain diagonal and transverse lines with liquid ulli, or rubber. For these squares there were twelve small stones, six red and six blue, which they divided among the players.

If two played, which was the ordinary way, one took six and the other the other six. Some large beans, patolli, from which the name is derived, usually five in number, used as dice with numbers painted on the surfaces were taken into both hands, shaken and thrown upon the mat by the players, and they would advance along the squares of the design as often times as the dice would indicate.

Several early anthropologists believed that many Asiatic influences were to be found in ancient Mexican life, and claimed that patolli bore a very close similarity to the Hindu game parchesi, further holding that patolli had been derived from the latter game.

They believed that playing backgammon-style, with colored stones as a counter, on a diagram like a cross full of squares on which the moves were made by counting squares according to the throws of marked lots, (in scoring with a disproportionate advantage given to the high throws), all corresponded to parchesi.

The player or team which first gained a certain score won the game. The total number which had to be covered by the player from the time he leaves until he returns to where he started, is fifty-two.

Therefore, patolli also had an astronomic religious significance, for the Mexican century consisted of precisely 52 years, as it results from the combination of the four signs, House, Rabbit, Reed, and Flint, with the numbers from oe to thirteen, four times thirteen equaling fifty-two.

The numbers that the board covers probably derived from the image of the sun, which, according to Aztec belief, passes through the fifty-two houses of the century.

The eagerness with which the Aztecs played this game, and how they addressed their dice with endearing terms and requests as though they were possessed with sense and intelligence is more than reminiscent to anyone who has witnessed a dice game during this era.

Even before actual play, they would prepare a fire and offer some food and incense to the dice and the playing-mat and to macuilxochitl, patron deity of the game. Then, the game would start with confidence and great anticipation.

After rubbing the beans for awhile between their hands, in the manner of our modern-day craps shooters, they would throw them on the mat with a loud cry and a great clap to maciulxochitl. A crowd of highly excited spectators would usually surround the players and take sides, gambling heavily on the outcome.

The Aztec calenderical system, which played a dominant role in the daily life of the Mexicans and in their ritual, consisted of the Tonalmatl, or sacred almanac of 260 days, used almost exclusively for ceremonial and divinatory computations, and for the fixing of certain "movable" feasts, and the solar years of 365 days, according to which the seasonal feasts were held.

In their measurement of time, they had established as their basis the "cempoualli," an artificial month composed of four weeks of five days each. The identity of their day was determined by a number and a sign. The numbers ran from one to thirteen, and then started all over again.

The signs, twenty in all, one for each day of the month, also followed each other concurrently, and were repeated each month. Thus the days of the first month were identified as follows:

1. Alligator.
2. Wind.
3. House.
4. Lizard.
5. Snails.
6. Death.
7. Deer.
8. Rabbit.
9. Water.
10. Dog.
11. Monkey.
12. Grass.

13. Reed.
1. Ocelot.
2. Eagle.
3. Vulture.
4. Motion.
5. Flint.
6. Rain.
7. Flowers.

The second month began with 8—Alligator, and so on.

It is curious that this Aztec calendar may be exactly illustrated with a modern deck of cards, laid out in rotation of the four suits, as an ace of hearts, two of spades, three of diamonds, four of clubs, five of hearts, etc. This system of combining signs with numerals is similar to that of Central Southwestern Asia, where among the Mongols, Tibetans, and Chinese, series of signs are thus combined to reckon years, months, and days.

We can elaborate on these signs in the following manner:

1. Alligator's head, or Cipactli. This sign is associated with fertility.

2. Ecatl. The head of the wind god representing instability.

3. Calli. A house, suggesting rest and associated with Tepeyollotl.

4. Lizard, or Queetzpolin, representing water and fertility.

5. Coatl. A snake's head, typifying poverty and homelessness.

6. Miquiztli. Representing the god of the underworld, associated with bad luck.

7. Mazatl. Head of a deer; implies timidity and misfortune.

8. Rabbit's head, or Tochtli. Associated with good luck and fertility.

9. Atl. Water. Symbolizes floods, death.

10. Dog's head, or Itzcuintli. Symbol of good fortune, rank, and riches.

11. Monkey's head, or Ozomatli. Implies cleverness and craftsmanship.

12. Grass, or Malinalli. Sometimes shown as a jawbone with grass hair. Misfortune.

13. Reed, or Acatl. Implies emptiness and bad luck.

14. Ocelot or jaguar. Success in war; death by sacrifice.

15. Eagle, or Quauhtli. Symbolizes courage.

16. Vulture, or Cozcoqualuhtli. Indicates old age.

17. Olin. Sign representing motion, earthquakes, inconstancy, change in fortune.

18. Stone knife, or Tecpatl. Symbol of drought and sterility.

19. Head of the god Tlaloc, or Quiauitl. Emblem of rain; unlucky sign.

20. Flower, or Xochitl. Suggesting good craftsmanship; bringer of good fortune.

After 260 days or 13 months have elapsed, the day known as 1—Alligator recurs, and the new cycle of 260 days which constitutes the astrological year or Tonalmatl begins again.

The solar or civil year consisted of 18 to 20 day months, plus a final period of 5 supernumerary days known as "nemontemi," or useless days. On these five extra days, which were looked upon as ill-omened and extremely unfortunate, a bare minimum or no work was done, the people rested and were generally inactive, went out as little as possible, made no transactions of importance, went out of their way to avoid quarreling. They also looked upon an evil omen encountered during this period as doubly unlucky.

No provision was made for intercalation, nor were corrections made for leap year, and so their calendar was gradually running behind the solar year. Therefore, it is quite obvious that a people, most of whose feasts were connected with agriculture, were bound to notice that their festivals gradually failed to correspond with the passing of the seasons. How they corrected for this is not yet known.

Each of the eighteen months had a special feast which was fixed, and each terminated with a spectacular flourish on the twenty-day period, and gave its name to that month. Each of these eighteen religious festivals was under the patronage of a special divinity, and each had a set of ceremonial rituals, peculiar to itself. In some instances, the many days of preparation were necessary ceremonies actually culminated.

The eighteen festivals can be described as follows:

1. Atlacualco—the first month dedicated to the Tlaloc rain gods, and Chalchihuilicue, a water goddess and the wife of the chief Tlaloc.

2. Tlacaxipevaliztli—the second month, dedicated to Xipe, god of flaying.

3. Tozoztontli, the third month, begun on March 14th, dedicated to the Tlalocs, coatlicue, a rain goddess and patroness of agriculture.

4. Huei Tozoztli, April 3, of the 4th month, dedicated to Centeotl, the maize god, and Chicomecoatl, goddess of maize.

5. Toxcatl—April 23, 5th month, dedicated to Tezcatlipoca, and at the festival held in his honor, the youth who had been impersonating him during the past year was sacrificed.

6. Etzaequaeiztli—May 13th, 6th month, symbolized by a figure of Tlaloc; ceremonies held in honor of the Tlalocs, and during the month, offerings of maize paste were made.

7. Tecuhilhuitontli—June 2nd, 7th month, highlighted by festivals held in honor of Huixtocihvatl, goddess of salt.

8. Hueitecuhilhiutl—June 22nd, 8th month, devoted to Xilonen, goddess of the tender ears of corn, which around this time were just beginning to ripen.

9. Tlaxuchimaco—July 12th, 9th month, dedicated to Huitzilopochtli, with the Aztec war god appearing on this occasion in benevolent guise.

10. Xocotlhuetzi—August 1st, 10th month, dedicated to a gruesome festival in honor of the fire god, Xiuhtecutli, or Huehueteotl, the "old, old, god."

11. Ochpaniztli—August 21st, 11th month, festivals in honor of Teteoinan, mother of the gods, also known as Tocitzin, and secondarily a goddess of the ripe maize.

12. Teotleco—September 10th, 12th month, symbolized by a figure of Tezcatlipoca, and celebrating the return of the gods who were believed to have been absent part of the year.

13. Tepeilhuitl—September 30th, 13th month, ushered in the festival of the mountain Tlalocs.

14. Quecholli—October 20th, 14th month, dedicated to Mixcoatl, God of Hunting.

15. Panquetzaliztli—November 9th, 15th month, distinguished by a great festival and ceremonial battle in honor of Huitzilopochtli, the Aztec war god.

16. Atemoztli—November 29th, 16th month, devoted to more festivals in honor of the Tlalocs, the rain and thunder gods of the mountains.

17. Tititl—December 19th, 17th month, marked by a feast in honor of Tlamatecuhtli, "the old princess."

18. Izcalli—January 8th, 18th month, dedicated to Xuihtecutli, the fire-god.

The ancient Mexicans also measured time in terms of long cycles, notably one of 52 years, and one of twice that period, 104 years. At the end of the period of time during which exactly seventy-three 260 day Tonalamatl or astronomical years had also expired, the same number and sign of the tonalamatl calendar again fell on the first day of the civil or solar year.

This event was looked upon by the Aztecs as very ominous for mankind, and was made the occasion of important ceremonies.

The Aztecs feared that the sun might fail to rise, and in the ensuing darkness, the Tzitzimiune would descend from the first heaven to plunge the world into destruction.

The principal feature of the ceremonies was the promise of the continuance of the world by the successful lighting of a new sacred fire, by means of the ceremonial fire sticks atop the mountain Uixachtlan, outside Mexico City at midnight.

This new fire gave promise of the gods that a new dawn would break, and the world would then continue to exist for another cycle of 52 years.

The tonalamatl, constituting the ritual and divinatory calendar, was the framework by which every arithmetical, chronological or astronomical observation could be determined positively. It was divided into twenty thirteen-day weeks.

The movable feasts of the ancient Aztecs, brief and comparatively minor, were mostly in definite relation to the tonalamatl, occurring on definite days, and were thus subject to repetition every 260 days.

This calendrical and astrological system formed a key part in the vast body of esoteric knowledge the study and elaboration of which the priests devoted so much of their attention. Numbers were invested with characteristics and mystical meanings. An elaborate mythology divided the history of the world into five ages, or "suns," each coming to an end in some great calamity—a future earthquake in the case of the present age.

This priestly cosmology placed Mexico at the center of the earth, and described in florid detail the thirteen heavens above, and nine hells below. Each of the four cardinal directions, to which were sometimes added the Zenith nadir, and middle, was associated with certain colors, gods, and day signs.

The Aztecs were familiar with certain stars in the heavens, having been attracted by their brilliance. To these stars, they attributed mysterious influences on the universe and mankind. Worshiping them therefore as divine forces, they watched with great care their movements across the night sky.

The chief duties of certain priests were astronomical observation, in addition to the supervision of the sacred fire which was kept burning continuously in the divine brazier of sculptured stone on top of each temple-crowned pyramid.

These priest-astronomers indicated the three divisions of the night by the sounding of drums and the burning of incense in honor of certain stars after twilight, at midnight, and at dawn.

Neetzahualpilli, one of the most enlightened tribal leaders of Texcoco (1470-1516), was known to be a great astrologer, priding himself on his knowledge of the motions of the celestial bodies. Each night, he was known to have ascended the terraced roof of his palace, along with his court astrologers, there to consider the stars, and contemplate their motions, relative positions, and thereby divine any hidden meanings therein.

The Aztec astrologers made systematic registration of the movements of celestial bodies in several different ways. They habitually employed not only their pyramid temples, but also their from dark chambers, located on a high point. One of the pictures found in the Mendoza Codex shows a seated high priest gazing upward at a symbol of the nocturnal heavens, depicted by a black semi-circle, studded with a number of eyes, for stars.

In addition, the astronomers used black obsidian mirrors extensively, for purposes of reflection as an aid to their work. Besides mirrors on the summit of temples and mountains, certain square columns placed on an elevation and faced with a broad band of obsidian mirrors can be found pictured in additional codices.

It is obvious that the latter, if carefully oriented, could have served as an excellent means of recording the periodical return of the planets, stars, and constellations to their former positions, reflected on the polished mirror surface as if in a frame.

After the election of Montezuma the second, he exhorted his people that he would make it his sworn duty to rise at midnight and look at the stars, especially at Yohualitqui Mamalhuaztli, as the Aztecs called the keys of St. Peter among the stars in the firmament, at the Citlaltlachtli, the north and its wheel, at the tiazquiztli, the Pleiades, and at the colotl ixaya, the constellation of the scorpion, which mark the four cardinal points in the sky.

Toward morning it would also be his duty to carefully observe the constellation Xonecuilli, what we call the cross of Saint Jacob, which appears in the southern sky in the direction of India and China; and he would carefully observe the "morning star," which appears at dawn and is called Tlanizcaepan teuctli.

These actions indicate the scope and principle elements of ancient Mexican astronomy, including the constellations, as well as the sun, moon, the Pleiades and morning star, the planet Venus, shooting stars and comets.

The early limited knowledge of medical remedies the Aztecs brought with them into the valley of Mexico expanded in proportion with their political and economic development as Tenochtitlan extended its military might, along with the infiltration of Aztec merchants into the Azpotec regions of Xoaxaca and into the southeastern part of Mexico where the Mayan speaking people were to be found. Trade relations with the Tarascans in Michoacán and the adjacent states and the exchange of contacts, brought knowledge of new flora and herbal medicines.

In addition to these herbs of medicinal value, they learned new methods of treatment which resulted in a hodge-podge mixture of ritualistic formulae linked with the gods and goddesses of different sections of Mexico.

We find that the religious concepts of the Aztecs cannot be disassociated from a discussion of their primitive medicine. Thus the ancient gods of the elements of the sun, the winds, rain, and storm, etc. were thought to bring the drought, lightning, rain, and floods which in turn were accompanied with certain diseases.

The gods of the earth who fostered the flowering of the crops and fecundity of the fauna also were responsible for the diseases that followed.

The belief existed that the gods possessed opposing dual attributes of both the dispenser and healer of disease. Ironically, the same god who meted out punishment to the unfortunate in the form of disease was also the patron of the physician and healer.

To illustrate with only a few examples: from the ancient omnipotent god Tezcatlipoca, the Aztecs conceived a goddess of medicine who dealt out diseases to the wicked. To another god of medicine, Ixtlilton, the natives made their offerings to prevent sickness befalling their children. Fathers taught their boys the chanting of incantations and sacred dances, which were an integral part of the ritual connected with this god.

Centeotl or Tonantzin, the earth goddess, also called Toci, regarded as the guardian of medicine and medicinal herbs, was worshiped especially by physicians, surgeons, midwives, and those capable of producing abortions by careful administration of herbs.

Quetzalcoatl, god of the air and wind, was responsible for the infirmities of catarrh and rheumatism, and was also believed to be capable of causing sterility in women. Likewise, the Tlalocs, Nahuatl, Amimitl, etc., also possessed the power to both convey and heal diseases.

Since it was within the province of the gods not only to dispense but also to cure diseases, one should not be surprised to find that many of the medicinal plants are named after gods and goddesses such as Capollaxipehualli—black cherry of Tipe—after Tipe, goddess of flaying; Cihuapahtli—female medicine—after Cihuacoatl; Cozcanantzi—jewel of Tonantzin—after Tonantzin, goddess of procreation; tlahcolteocacatl—herb of Tlahcalteotl—goddess of sexual intercourse.

Some of the names of other plant remedies were associated with the word teotl, meaning god, sacred, or divine. For instance there is to be found in the Index of the Badianus Manuscript reference to teoamatl—sacred paper; teonochtli—sacred nopal; teoxihuitl—sacred plant; teoyztaquilitl—sacred white edible plant.

The astronomical signs of the zodiac associated with signs of the Aztec calendar were used by the Aztecs to denote various anatomical areas as well as certain physiological phenomena. For example, the 20 days of the Mexican month corresponded to the different parts of the human body as follows:

Cipactli—alligator—liver
ehecatl—wind—respiration
calli—house—right eye
cuetzpallin—lizard—gut
coatl—snake—sexual organs
miquiztli—death—head
mazatl—deer—right leg
tochtli—rabbit—left auricle
atl—water—scalp
itzcuintli—dog—nostrils
ozmatli—monkey—left arm
malinalli—herb—intestine
ocatl—reed—stomach
ocelotl—jaguar—left leg
cuantli—eagle—right arm
cozcocuauhtli—vulture—right ear

ollintonatiuh—tongue—movement
techpatl—stone—teeth
quiahuitl—rain—left eye
ochitl—flower—nipple

Prior to the coming of the Spaniards, all cases of sickness among the Aztecs were handled by several kinds of physicians: the true curanderos, the tepate, the sorcerer, the tieitl, as well as fortune tellers, jugglers and magicians proper.

Very often, the family of the ill person would call in all types of physicians since divination was expected to reveal the cause of sickness. The feeling was that if any of the latter did no good, they would do no harm, either.

The ancient Mexicans, like most primitive peoples, did not attribute sickness to natural causes. It might be due to lack of sufficient homage to a deity, punishment for some wrong, or the sorcery of an enemy. After the diviner discovered the cause of the illness, counter magic would then be used. Most practitioners would chant ritualistic formulae, administer charms, and generally rely on mystical powers to aid in the recovery.

They were reported to have employed in their invocations and chants a dialect or mode of speech which differed from that in common use, and calculated to throw an additional air of solemnity on their expressions. This speech bore evident traces of archaic forms and obsolete terms, indicating that it was a survival of a more ancient stratum of the language of the tribe.

The true physician, who it was believed obtained his knowledge of healing from certain deities of the Mexican pantheon attempted to relieve suffering manually or through pharmaceutical means.

Women were trained as doctors as well as men, both in the art of sorcery as well as healing. These women were well versed in the knowledge and preparation of herbs, trees, and stones, how to bleed the patient, give physic, administer medicines, rub the body to soften up hardened parts, set bones, clean and cure ulcers, gout, diseases of the eye, and cut out fleshy growths.

There were women, trained in sorcery, who were regarded as evil. They were thought to have made pacts with demons, knew how to prepare drinks which killed, and instead of curing, they were thought to put in danger the life of all those who were ill. Who employed these doctors can be left to the imagination.

They were known to employ trickery to obtain their ends, by, for example, blowing upon the painful part, tying and untying various strings, gazing on water and throwing the grains of corns used in her divinations, pretending to extract worms from teeth, and paper and flint from other parts of the body.

In extracting all this, she would announce that she was destroying the illness. The patient's demise would soon follow.

The Conquistadors were impressed by the medical knowledge of the Aztecs and wrote about it in praiseworthy terms in their early reports. In addition to their dependence on medical treatments by pharmaceutical herbs, the Aztecs believed in preventive medicine through proper hygienic practices.

The numerous references to the care of the teeth in the early chronicles indicated that the Nahuans gave considerable attention to their condition.

For example, the Conquistadors quoted the Aztecs as follows: "In order to avoid diseases of the teeth, it is well to avoid eating very hot food. If hot food is eaten, do not drink very cold water immediately after eating; also employ a wooden toothpick. Use warm water and salt for cleaning the teeth, and rub them frequently with a cloth and some finely-ground charcoal."

Lack of cleanliness, damp atmosphere, excess dust, extremes of cold and heat, and all forms of dissipation were also recognized as possible causes for diseases as well as punishment imposed by a cruel god. Bathing in the form of cold outdoor baths or steam baths within the sweat-houses, temazcalli, with massage, constituted a significant part of the health and personal hygiene of the native Mexicans. Just as popular were also the warm sulfur baths in neighboring hills.

The medicinal use of the fragrance of flowers for their psychic effect as a mild stimulant in the treatment of fatigue, fever, and melancholia, was also recognized.

The Aztecs were also familiar with surgical practices. Their skill in delicate operations, and their use of antiseptics, narcotics, pain relief and bone-setting, the use of surgical instruments, all point to evidence of a considerable knowledge of the body and its functions.

Medical remedies were usually of complex formulae consisting principally of various plant extracts to which were added earth and diverse stones as well as parts of animals.

The wide use of parts of animals or their blood as well as the specific naming of the animals in each remedy suggested some symbolic connection or sympathetic magic between the animal and the type of ailment.

In addition to the use of substances of animal origin, the Aztecs used a wide range of crystals, earth pigments, different kinds of soils, minerals, and precious stones, as antidotes for all kinds of ailments, looking upon them as possessing a magical as well as therapeutic value.

The materials of plant origin used by the Aztecs for medicinal purposes covered a wide range of forms, with an ecological range from the tropics through the temperate, to the high cold mountainous regions. It seems that the ancient Mexicans looked upon the plants as possessing a spirit like that of animals or even man himself.

Certain plants were signaled with honors while others were shunned with great fear. Still others were given little attention since they were regarded as neutral—possessing no pronounced virtues or evil properties.

Some of those venerated highly by the Aztecs were the narcotic plant ololiuhqui, and numerous other species of the genus Datura; the extract of the peyote known as teonanoctl, was also widely used by the Aztecs to produce hallucinations.

From these plants, the native physicians made use of narcotics, purgatives, emetics, diuretics, hemostatics, tonics, expectorants, antipyretics, astringents, and antispasmodics.

From Torquemada we learn that Montezuma kept a garden of medicinal herbs, and that his court physicians experimented with them and attended the nobility.

Common people rarely saw these doctors for medical aid, because a fee was charged for their services, and the medicinal value of herbs was common knowledge. In many instances, people could concoct remedies from their own gardens. These simple household remedies prepared in various crude forms from the common herbs of the garden or fields at large were common knowledge to most members of a family, acquired as part of normal home training.

The Aztecs were well acquainted with insect lore, (far more so than most of us who dwell in cities today), and saw them as foods as well as poisonous creatures whose stings possessed properties that could be beneficial to therapeutic treatments. In many cases, they recognized the different kinds of insects, such as ants, classified them according to their habits, and the intensity of their bite, sting, or utility.

The profession of medicine in ancient Mexico was kept within a guild, just like the various other skilled occupations, and with them, their trade secrets accumulated, and their knowledge of herbal medicine expanded with the passing of years.

At certain centers in the neighborhood of Tenochtitlan, such as Coyoacan, Texcoco, and Huaxtepec, large herb gardens were cultivated and maintained by the chieftains of these districts. These lords encouraged the training of men skilled in gardening and in the extraction and use of the herbs.

These latter would also experiment with the plants, engage in the practice of medicine, and quite frequently would offer instruction in the art of healing to their apprentices.

Involved in a so-called course of study for the true profession of physician among the Aztecs, (and this perhaps is simplifying matters too readily), would be a mastery of their known knowledge of medical and surgical pathology, therapeutics, botany and pharmacy.

A master's knowledge of pharmacy alone would require the learning of the history of plants, their geographical distribution, a classification involving their distinctive characteristics, all their known properties, to be followed by a thorough grounding in the combinations of formulae made up of various ingredients ranging from the many simple officially sanctioned medications, to the most elaborate of compounds.

8

Agricultural, Commercial and Vocational Pursuits of the Aztecs

Opposed to the bloody side of the picture of ancient Mexican life obtained from the early chronicler's accounts of their many wars and accompanying sacrifices to their ever-demanding gods, we have a picture of peaceful pursuit of daily occupations and trades, revealing that many of the Aztecs were content to leave war to the professional soldiery, even though they themselves could be called into service at any time of need.

Along the east and west coasts of Mexico there extends a narrow strip of level land known as "tierra caliente," distinguished by a tropical climate, steamy jungle forest fauna and flora. Continuing further inland, climbing three thousand feet above sea level, the temperate or sub-tropical zone ("tierratemplada") is found on the outer slopes of the mountains.

A wedge-shaped plateau, seventy five hundred feet in height, constituting the geographical backbone of Mexico, and known as the cold country or "tierra fria," covers the area between the two converging mountain ranges, the eastern and western Sierra Madre.

It was in the temperate and fertile valley of Mexico, also rich in minerals, that the Aztecs lived. Covering seventeen hundred square miles, it lay like an oval bowl surrounded by mountains of the Anahuac range, bordered on the north by the Sierra de Tzontlapan and the higher Pachuca range, on the northwest by the foothills of Cerro de Sincoque and Cerro de Talpan, to the west by the Sierra de Monte Alto and Monte Bajo, on the southwest by the Monte de las Cruces.

Southward rises the Sierra de Ajusco and to the southeast are the Iztaccihualt, the "white-woman," and Papocatepetl. On the eastern fringe is the great salt lake Txcoco, and to the south lie the fresh water lakes of Xochimilco and Chalco which provide shallow basins for a wide number of different types of aquatic and moisture-loving plants. The summers in this region were cool, and the winters rarely brought snow and frosts, although chill winds were common.

During the four months of June through September, irregular, severe storms caused a rainy season, while the dry season began with October and was of an eight-month duration.

The changes wrought in the appearance of the Valley of Mexico by the alternating dry and wet seasons were truly cataclysmic. During the latter part of the month of May the rains would come and by June the dull colored hills and plateaus turned green and exploded into color.

There followed a succession of blooms which carried on into December, quite some time after the last of the rains had come to a halt. It was during the height of the dry spell that the wooded timberland of the mountains yielded the moisture and protective shade necessary for the maturation and blossoming of many varieties of plants common to northern climates.

While mining ranked as an industry of importance among the Aztecs for the extraction of gold, silver, copper, obsidian, and precious stones, the real wealth of the ancient Aztecs was based almost entirely on agriculture. Everybody, including the inhabitants of the metropolis, with the exception of the professional soldiery and the great nobles, cultivated the soil.

Since farming amounted practically to an almost universal occupation, merely varying in degrees of extent, all children had to undergo a period of learning how to till the soil. This learning however, consisted of more than the mere acquisition of basic knowledge which farming demanded. Civic and religious institutional duties were also closely interwoven in it, as they were with every occupational calling in all of ancient Mexico.

One of the first tasks usually assigned to a young boy was the keeping guard over the growing and ripening maize in a sheltered station overlooking the field for the purpose of driving away with stones and shouts many flocks of feathered "robbers" which abounded in the country. The children were also made to help the men in the lighter work of the field such as scattering the seeds, weeding the plants, and husking and cleaning the corn.

Concerning the particular methods of cultivation practiced by the Aztecs which the boys had to learn, we find very little definite information in the early chronicles, except on the raising of maize.

In the plateau country which was relatively treeless, the soil was evidently made ready for sowing with hoes, since the plow was not yet in existence in the new world before the coming of the Europeans. In preparing the lowland soil for cultivation, the trees and brush were first cut down, then burned, the ashes serving, so far as is known, as their only fertilizer.

The removal of the trees before planting could start was a laborious undertaking because of the density of the tropical forest, and the fact that the natives possessed no better tool than a stone axe. They then enclosed their fields with stone walls and hedges of maguey, which were kept in good condition and carefully repaired each year in the month of Panquetzaliztli.

Cattle, horses, pigs or sheep were not to be found in ancient Mexico. Some have taken this absence of domesticated animals as proof of the barbarous state of old Mexican civilization, seemingly forgetting that one cannot domesticate a non-existing animal, and the Mexicans themselves domesticated various fowl and dogs, as well as several species of non-venomous snakes.

The lack of domestic beasts of burden thus affected greatly Mexican agriculture, making work in the field an extremely laborious task with the aid of only a few primitive farming implements: a kind of wooden shovel or spade in the operation of which both hands and feet were used; a coatl or hoe of copper, with a wooden handle used to break the surface of the soil; and another instrument made of copper and wood like a sickle, and usually used for pruning fruit trees.

In the Osuna Codex, a Mexican laborer is shown using a kind of wooden shovel, the name of which is huitli or coanactl. In the Mendoza Codex this tool can be seen with a basket (chiquinitl) with a broad carrying strap placed over the wrist or shoulder.

Over the ash-covered soil the planters would pass, making holes with a sharpened stick at intervals of about three feet, into which three or four kernels of corn were dripped and then covered with earth by foot. Care was taken to make the rows perfectly straight and uniform.

The field was kept clean of weeds and at different times steps were taken to ensure the growth of the stalks by such means as supporting them by heaping up the soil around them, and at maturity breaking the stalk two-thirds up so that the hanging ear might be protected from the rain by the husks.

It was customary in many parts of the land for groups numbering even as many as twenty men to join together for the purpose of helping each other in the job of preparing and sowing the crops.

Apart from those times when they worked communally for the purpose of helping each other, the men of each calpulli had a civic responsibility in tilling jointly the altepetlalli for the raising of civic expenses for special public reasons, to raise tribute, to furnish military supplies, to maintain the temples, the sacerdotal order and religious service, the local chieftains, and lastly for the entertainment of official visitors.

As with all other occupations there were certain religious rites and observances which accompanied the manual work in the field. The introduction to these became a necessary part of a boy's mastering farming practices.

To ascertain the appropriate day of sowing, soothsayers would be called in to consult the sacred almanac called the Tonalmatl. The seed was procured from certain ears of corn of the preceding harvest which had been blessed at special ceremonies in the temple of Chicomecoatl, a goddess of maize, at the feast held in the fourth month Huei Totzozontli.

It seems that the ancient Mexicans believed that Chicomecoatl lie concealed in these ears of corn which were stored in the house since the blessing.

As the farmer left for the field, he would entreat the bag in which the seed had been placed, and his planting stick, to give him aid in his work. He would also make supplication to the soil to yield a rich harvest.

Occasionally, a local priest would put in an appearance at the sowing, and consent to scatter the seed on the ground to the accompaniment of a prayer. The Tlalocs were also called upon at this juncture to protect the newly sown crop from animals that might uproot the seeds or inflict any other damage upon it.

The religious precautions did not close at this point. Shortly after several weeks had passed and the plants had made their appearance above ground, overtures were again made to the gods of rain with the burning of a candle of beeswax and an offering of copal incense. Then, later, when the ears began to form, the sacrifice would be a turkey, and the candles and copal offered this time to Chicomecoatl.

The corn was to be left untouched until the silk made its appearance, and as soon as it did, a number of ears were picked off together with green leaves and the first flowers of maize, and brought to the storehouse, where in company with the customary turkey, copal and beeswax candle, they were offered in thanks.

Where the green corn was found to be edible, additional sacrificial offerings, this time of some of the corn, were made on altars on the hill tops. There, at first, observances would be made to the fire god, Xiuhtecutli. Then copal would be scattered on the fire after which the green ears were placed to roast.

Occasionally, some of the more zealous observers would prick themselves and draw blood, which was sprinkled with some pulque on the roasting corn.

Other types of sacrificial offerings included paper anointed with crude rubber, and this was for the rain gods, the Tlalocs. Special ceremonies of celebration were observed when a maize plant produced two or three ears, a rarity to the Aztecs, since the maize of those days could not have been anywhere as highly developed as the modern plant.

The use of their primitive machinery was obviated to some degree by the richness of the soil, which even now in some regions permits three harvestings in a year. Although they did not obtain from the land as much produce as the soil was capable of yielding, however, the extent of cultivation made a great harvest possible.

They were acquainted with the principle of irrigation, tapping and diverting the water of rivers and mountain streams by means of canals, ditches and dams. They also frowned upon indiscriminate and wanton destruction of their woods, setting up severe penalties.

Huge storehouses in which their maize was kept after harvests were usually to be found close to their dwellings. Theses granaries, admitted by the Conquistadors to be of admirable construction, were built of the long, tough, flexible branches of the oyametl tree, laid in log-house fashion to make a compact square room with a water-tight roof, and with only an opening at the top and bottom.

Some of these barns were built large enough to hold many thousands of bushels, and corn could be stored and preserved in them for many years.

In addition to the raising of maize, the principle crop and chief food of the natives, there was another food plant of considerable importance—a species of amaranth—a grain smaller than mustard seed and known to the Aztecs as huahutli, which, once gathered, insured the people to a great extent against possible famine should the maize crop be blighted.

Other staple products of the Valley of Mexico, the method of planting and nurturing of which had to be learned by the farmer boy, included potatoes, chili peppers of great variety, tomatoes, beans, squash, and calabasa, a special class of turnip.

In addition to the regular farming areas where the staple products were raised, gardens beautifully planned, were common. Large quantities of native fruits such as the banana, mango, pineapple, avocado, guava, zapote, and chirimoya, along with scores of others, were cultivated in special gardens and made up of a very important part of the daily diet of the native population.

There were others devoted to the cultivation of vegetables, medicinal and aromatic herbs, flowers, native roses, and trees with fragrant blossoms, of which there were many kinds. The Aztecs used flowers on every possible religious and secular occasion.

The flower was for the Mexicans, an emblem of the beautiful—and contributed to the enjoyment of life, color, fragrance, taste, art, and artistic skill, music, and sport, but above all, love and even sexual indulgence—all was in the imagination of the Mexicans associated with the picture of the flower.

The use of flowers on all possible occasions is a beautiful custom which has persisted in Mexico even until today. The very poorest will buy flowers as often as possible. They marry with them. There are the yellow cempasuchil for the dead. They cure the sick with flowers. Before the household "santo," together with the colored oil lamp, are fresh flowers. Men, women, and children wear floral wreaths when they attend the special festivals of miraculous saints. They received honored guests with flowers. Lovers present them to their sweethearts and parents.

Cervantes de Salazar, one of the 16th century chroniclers, devoted a chapter of his work to Montezuma's gardens, and marveled at the skill of the gardeners who with much art and delicacy could construct a thousand figures of persons by means of leaves and flowers, and also the seats, chapels and other structures which adorned the gardens.

The "hanging gardens" of Montezuma which were found at the top of a hill of Chapultepec, was a tribute to the Aztec wisdom and skill as gardeners, demonstrating that they had learned from long experience that many plants thrive best among rocks which not only preserve moisture, but also the heat of the sun, which counteracted the chilliness of the night temperature in that high altitude.

A story worth relating for the information contained therein concerns Montezuma II, and his efforts to restore and build up the tropical gardens at Huaxtepec, located south of the Valley of Mexico, which he had inherited from his predecessor and namesake, Montezuma, the Elder, at the time of his rise to the chieftainship of the Aztecs, circa 1450.

After his installation as ruler, he sent his principal overseer, Pinotetl, with orders to inspect and restore the fountains and springs, the streams, reservoirs, and irrigation systems.

Simultaneously, he dispatched messengers to the tropical coast region with a request to the lord of Cuetlaxtla for plants with roots of the vanilla orchid, the cacao and magnolia trees, and various other vegetable products; with foresight, he also asked that these be brought carefully by native gardeners from the same region, capable of replanting them at the proper season, and tending them in the most propitious way.

On receiving his message, the lord of Cuetlaxtla immediately gave orders to have a number of all kinds of plants dug with their roots enclosed in earth, and with exquisite courtesy, he had these bundles wrapped in beautifully woven mantas, and dispatched to Mexico.

The ceremonials observed by the gardeners who accompanied them before the planting, is worth mentioning here. They fasted for eight days, and drawing blood from the helix of their ears, they anointed the plants therewith. Asking Pinotetl, (Montezuma II's overseer) for a quantity of incense, rubber and paper, they also made a great sacrifice to the god of flowers, offering him many dead quail after having sprinkled the plants, and the soil around them with their blood.

They assured the people that after observing these ceremonies none of the plants would be lost, and that they would soon bear flowers and fruits. Their predictions were fulfilled, and before three years had passed, all of their charges blossomed luxuriantly.

Bernal Diaz Adel Castillo, in his account of Cortes' second expedition to Mexico refers to Montezuma II's gardens as "The finest I have ever seen in all my life." Indeed, Cortes himself, in his Third Letter to Charles V, dated May 15, 1522, described them as, "The finest, most pleasant, perhaps the largest gardens ever seen, having a circumference of at least two leagues ..."

When we review our knowledge of agriculture among the Aztecs, we find that the skills to be acquired by the Aztec youngsters in the different branches of agriculture would usually be dependent upon the father's own specialty in food or flower planting. This could range all the way from gardening for the Montezumas, as we have seen, to the cultivation of cacao beans, or the maguey, for all its different by-products.

The most providential plant was the aforementioned maguey, or agave. It had almost unlimited uses, including the production of wine (pulque), vinegar, honey, sweet-meats (arrope), cloth for men and women, cordage, beams for houses, shingles for covering them, needles for sewing, etc.

The maguey, both wild and cultivated, served many other purposes. It was used for the manufacture of paper, the dry blades for the feeding of fires, the thorns for use as nails and awls. Its hollows held rain water as in a deposit created by nature itself.

It seems natural then, for the Aztecs to regard the agave or maguey as a wonder of the vegetable kingdom. When they recognized the benefits the plant conferred on them, there seemed good ground for the generalization that without the plant, along with their maize, the great population and civilization of the high plateau of Mexico would have been impossible.

What electricity and fibre-optics are to modern civilization, the fibres of the agave were to ancient Mexican culture. No country had a greater variety of material for cordage or textiles then was furnished to the Mexican tribes by the agave and its related indigenous plants.

With every step the Aztecs took in their advancement, this plant became more useful. The cultivation of cereals derived from this and other plants, became indispensable to the well-being of the Aztec nation.

From their beginnings in the Valley of Mexico, the industrial arts of the Aztecs were of a domestic nature, intended to satisfy the needs for the direct conservation of the group. In an agrarian society like theirs, a knowledge of all the handicrafts which did not demand great skill or ingenious instruments was mastered by every Indian. Being possessors of an exceptional political genius, however, they rose to the heights of military power.

This military ascendancy, which brought in its wake an expansion through conquest and commerce, and subsidized their industrial arts, along with the ensuing refinements of luxury which roused their aesthetic feelings, made their capital city the center of Mexican civilization at the time of the Spanish Conquest.

A natural outcome of conquest is tribute, and the tribute exacted by the Aztecs from the many tribes they conquered, as far removed as the Huaxtec of northern Vera Cruz, and the Maya of Guatemala, played an important role in their development. Since the state of Aztec agriculture was made secure further by the receipt of additional agricultural produce as part of their tribute, the development of their industrial arts was able to grow apace.

Tribute determined also, a kind of industrial specialization for the subjected regions. Each was expected to offer up a certain amount of their own products either in their original state or in a modified form of manufacture. Each district therefore progressed in the cultivation and transformation of its native natural resources.

The raw materials obtained by the Aztecs in large quantities, also gave impetus to the manufacture of certain articles in their towns.

Growth in commerce was another determining factor in the industrial development of the Aztecs. Originally, with an active traffic with the neighboring tribes of the lake, their commerce widened with the expansion of the activities of the Aztec merchants who began to penetrate into provinces inhabited by other tribes.

The Aztec merchants occupied an important role in the social scale of Ancient Mexico and were the recipients of much consideration and privileges from the body politic. These merchants were grouped into a guild which has been compared to a religious order, because of its strong cohesion, its peculiar rites, ceremonies, and customs.

The Aztec word for merchant, "tlanamacanti," denotes "a man who exchanges one thing for another," and hence, every artisan who bartered his own manufactures in the market places, for whatever he desired for his upkeep, was in a certain sense, a merchant.

The true merchant, however, was a sort of wandering trader, who aspired to a wealth greater than the satisfying of immediate needs, and who made a business of importing and exporting whatever he could gather from within and outside of his own environs. This exclusive enterprise carried the Aztec merchant to the farthest extremes of Mexico, and to the distant tribes touching the borders of Anahuac.

The regions that lie to the south were looked upon as being rich markets for valued and rare products, slaves, and raw materials which latter could be transformed in turn at home into new articles for consumption and exchange.

Expeditions of these traders traveled through towns along the seashore, and the interior. There was not a place they did not pry into and visit, buying and selling their wares. It was neither too hot nor too cold for their travel and activities. Whatever they found that was pretty, valuable, practical or advantageous, they bought and sold.

A universal metallic specie was lacking, and probably this factor helped considerably in maintaining a steady traffic in the diffusion of goods. It is true, however, that apart from their barter, the Aztecs did recognize some things which passed as money or currency, and that, in exactness, gave the exchange the aspect of a modern buying and selling exchange.

For example, a close study of the available early sources of this period reveals the mention of the existence and use of five different classes of money. Gold, in grains or dust, was one of these, and was generally handled in transparent duck quills which enabled one to see at a glance the quantity contained.

The size of the quill was the measure of value. Another standard of value in commerce was cotton cloth, cut in small pieces, colored and stamped, and called patolquachtli, and was used in making purchases of the utmost necessity. Frequently, pieces of tin were also used as a medium of exchange. Copper, another form of money, much of which has been preserved, was cut and hammered into pieces in the form of a chopping knife, resembling somewhat the letter T.

The money used, most widely, and for the larger transactions in commerce, was cacao. This was not the bean called tlalcacahuatl, or small cacao, with which they made their chocolate drinks, but a more common specie known as patlacchte, and less likely to be served as a food. Its use was practically confined to mercantile transactions. The numerical system of the ancient Mexicans based the count of the cacao beans upon the number twenty.

Four hundred grains, twenty by twenty, made up on zontle. Twenty zontles or eight thousand, were the equivalent of one Xiquipilli, and three of these Xiquipillis made up a cargo, or load, having twenty four thousand grains of cacao. To avoid the annoyance of counting all these out during a sale of extremely valuable merchandise, sacks of recognized sizes, such as sacks of eight thousand, or half sacks of four thousand were used.

These early traders suffered great hardships, and were extremely daring; they went anywhere, even an enemy's domain, and were sly in their dealings with strangers, being sure to learn their languages as well as their tactics. Often, they assumed the dress of the particular province, in order not to be regarded as strangers.

They made sure to find out where the precious stones and feathered plumes could be had, or the gold, then purchased them, and took them to where they were worth a great deal on resale. They also knew where to find exquisite and valuable skins of beasts, and where to resell them at high prices. Likewise did they deal in precious cups of many different kinds and material, adorned with diverse painted figures, some of which had covers made of tortoise shell, and spoons of the same, to stir the cocoa.

These trading expeditions, because of their nature, were always very hazardous undertakings, and demanded a special organization. The journey was made by groups of merchants of similar rank traveling together, with a large body of attendants of lower rank who were hired for the purpose of transporting the commodities.

The whole company was equipped with arms, and precautions were taken to guard against surprise attacks. They went usually so well prepared that they were able to maintain a defense strong enough to withstand hostilities until reinforcements arrived from home.

While the members of the expedition were to be of a sufficient number to withstand the attacks of hostile and marauding bands, they were not, however, to seem so numerous as to excite suspicion. In spite of their being well-armed, they were to be extremely cautious in their endeavors to avert friction.

The porters, whose average weight of burden consisted of fifty to sixty pounds of merchandise and supplies, and covered about fifteen miles on a day's march, were not to be too numerous.

The most successful merchants thus came to assume importance in community standing, not only because of their amassed wealth, and because of the finding of distant markets for the industries of their tribe, but also for the reason that their peculiar calling could often furnish the Aztec warlords with convenient excuses for declaring war on bordering provinces, enabling them to extend the Mexican sphere of influence, and exact new tribute.

Thus, the merchant was the forerunner of the warrior; commerce initiating that which conquest was later to realize.

Mexican trade was thus promoted into a most prosperous state, and protected by the Aztec chieftains. In one famous example, In the wild forests of Mictlan-quauhtla, some inhabitants of the city of Uaxyacac murderously attacked and plundered a Mexican caravan which was returning home from Tabasco with costly goods.

The king then reigning, Motecuhzoma the elder, equipped an expedition to avenge the deaths, and the crime was avenged by the total annihilation of the entire offending tribe.

A number of Mexican families of about six hundred families from neighboring cities situated in the Valley of Mexico, started out to settle the now-vacant lands of the exterminated tribe, under the leadership of four Mexican chieftains, whom the king had chosen for his expedition.

Assault and assassination of Mexican merchants are almost always cited as the "causi belli" in the native records, as the reasons for going to war.

There must have been an apprenticeship for the occupation of merchant (that is, for the sons of the latter, since the guild was a closed one), for he had to acquire some knowledge of geography and skill in painting of maps in order to trace the plan of the roads and lakes over which they passed. He had to become an intrepid explorer, and break new trails.

As a frequent ambassador of the reigning chieftain, he had to master all the requisites of diplomatic ceremony, and to take the necessary steps for establishing amicable political and economic relations. A thorough mastery of arms and war tactics was essential to all engaged in such dangerous enterprises.

As they made their way from village to village, exchanging their articles for others not manufactured at home, frequently hostile bands would waylay them. At times, even in the midst of the neighborly attitude of a distant fair, treachery could rear its head with wholesale butchery as the end.

The apprentice found that he had to become a linguist, and had to learn the languages and dialects of the people on his route. He became a sociologist to a certain extent, when he had to learn how to cultivate the friendship of the inhabitants of the different villages, and mingle with them, adopt their mode of dress, and make a study of their resources, habits, and customs.

Being in an excellent position to obtain important and desirable information concerning the state and resources of the enemy provinces, he had to adopt the subtle attributes which make for successful spying.

It was necessary, furthermore, for the apprentice to learn the duties of a fiscal agent for the chief and state, since he demanded and obtained payment of tribute at the various stopping-places on his long treks. Finally, a knowledge of his wares, and of his markets, and of the principles of salesmanship and bartering had to be gained.

Apart from the latter instructions, the apprentice had also to learn the different ways of honoring "Yacatecutli," the lord of travelers, who had been adopted as divinity of the merchant's guild, because it was believed that he was the first one who had started trading among them.

As the god who watched over the traveling tradesmen, he was honored in the form of a bamboo traveler's staff. The tradesmen paid great honor to this. Wherever they went, whatever country they entered for trading purposes, they took their staff with them; at whatever spot on the road they made camp for the night, they placed the staff in an upright position, and performed their religious rites before it, drawing their own blood, and offering it, along with copal, to their god Yacatecutli.

Once on the road, the merchants were quick to detect signs and omens which would foretell the success or failure of their venture, placing much stock on their import. One omen which they particularly heeded was the singing of a bird named oactli, in two different ways.

Each manner conveyed a message: one to lift their hearts; the other a dreaded one of bad omen. If they heard the bird-song of evil portent, they turned to each other, knowing that some evil might come to them. The rising of a river might carry them or their merchandise away, or they might fall into the hands of robbers; perhaps they might be eaten by wild beasts, or be met with hostilities.

Whereupon their chief, walking amongst them, would remind them that it was not proper that they should become frightened, for they knew full well when they left their homes that such calamities might befall them. They knew they were about to offer themselves to death, and they had seen the tears and lamentations of their relatives, who had given them to understand that in some faraway mountain they might leave their bones and spill their blood. Now the omen had come to pass and it was not proper Aztec behavior that anyone should become faint-hearted. Instead, they should prepare to die like men. He then would exhort them to pray, and not indulge in weakness.

He reminded them of their glory and fame, and of what they owed to their superiors and predecessors, the noble and estimable merchants from whom they descend. He reminded them that they were not the first, nor should they be the last, to whom these misfortunes would happen; many before and many after would find themselves in the same position; therefore they must take heart and courage, and be brave men.

In order to avert the impending disaster, certain rites were, however, observed when they prepared to camp that night, wherever it might happen to be. Uniting all their traveler's staffs, they tied them in a bundle, called this the image of the god of merchants, Yacatecutli. In front of this bundle of staffs, they then drew blood from their ears, with great humility and reverence.

Piercing their tongues, they passed twigs of willow through them, and offered these, covered in blood, to the bundle. This was in token of their resolution to bear in patience any evil that their god might inflict upon them.

Having performed this act of submission, they sought to dismiss the matter from their minds, and to meet their fate calmly; only those few who were timid might continue to meditate upon it in fear.

An expedition returning safely to Tenochtitlan was always greeted joyously, and the welcome extended to it was only outdone by that accorded to the tribal warriors returning from a successful campaign or raid. Immediately upon arriving, the traders went to the main temple to make their worship to their gods and offer thanks for their safe homecoming.

The group next met the tribal council and the leading warriors, either in open meeting in the presence of the populace, or, if considered wiser, in secret conclave, to recount the results of their venturous undertaking. Later, they went to their particular quarters to be received in an appropriate manner of celebration. On some occasions, the whole tribe would turn out to celebrate with ceremonial dancing and a general feast.

Certain factors prevented an immediate substantial profit from these trading expeditions, and they must be taken into consideration. Whatever they brought back with them, in merchandise and tribute, had to be carried by men, and the number of these assistants had to be restricted as mentioned above, in order not to imperil the object of their precarious undertaking by arousing undue suspicion along the way.

Since it was also necessary for the porters to carry a safe margin of provisions and supplies to offset any possible dearth of food because of lack of success in hunting and the passing through uncultivated regions, deserts and wilderness, the amount of articles and materials brought home, even though of extreme value, was limited.

Profits were distributed, also, in a certain proportion to the tribe, temples, and quarters, and to the merchants themselves; but their greatest reward came in the bestowing of marks of distinction and privileges. These raised them to a position of outstanding warriors, and often, to high rank within the tribe.

In recognition of their importance to the tribe, they were permitted to adopt insignia and devices of their own, to have their own courts in which civil and criminal cases were tried, and to enjoy the prestige which their wealth and courage brought them.

On every fifth day, open market was held, and from great distances the produce and manufactures were brought, and the broad roads leading to the main markets or to the local ones in the provinces were punctuated by resting places for the wayfarers and carriers at set intervals.

Distance for the Aztec was thus measured by the number of these resting places between one point and another. In order to prevent fraud and confusion, no sale except in ordinary edibles, could be made on the highway or elsewhere outside of the market, under threat of severe penalties.

Each particular kind of merchandise was placed on display for sale on a site designated by the judges of commerce presiding in state over the fair, and no articles were to be sold in any other places than those already set aside for them.

In addition to the judges there were other officers who maintained order and directed the traffic. Standard measures were observed, and severe punishment was meted out to any who attempted to sell by false measure or exchange stolen goods. Traders, of bulky articles, such as lumber and stones, were permitted to place their wares on sites on the canal or adjacent streets.

The evidence of the industrial life of the Aztecs found in the market of the capital city, reflected the various phases of their social organization.

Manual skill was esteemed highly, and the different trades to be found in Aztec society were grouped into orders resembling guilds. There were, to enumerate just a few, workers in gold, silver, and copper, expert lapidaries, woodcarvers, potters, cloth manufacturers, dye and paint makers, paper makers, feather artists, soap and torch firms, builders and architects.

These guilds were not, however, like the brotherhoods or guilds of medieval Europe, which had been set up by the working classes for mutual protection from the violence and extortions of the nobility and clergy. The Aztec guilds were hereditary in nature, and many of them were made up mainly of Toltec families which had persisted ever after the breakup of the Toltec empire.

Some of their more highly developed arts and crafts, with their secrets of design composition, decoration, and construction, had usually been perpetuated in a special clan composed of a group of families bound by a common descent, passing from father to son until the work became even more increasingly specialized and refined, producing articles of remarkable delicacy which demanded great skill, the collaboration of many persons, and an immense pride in what they were doing.

Their manner and methods of working at times, were painstakingly slow, resulting always in a truly admirable piece of work. Patience, attentiveness, and perseverance were necessary attributes which had to be cultivated, to lead to an assured success in workmanship.

Their feather work was sometimes so sophisticated and complex that if there were twenty artisans, they would undertake jointly the manufacture of one piece, dividing among themselves the figure of the image in as many parts as there were of their number, each one taking his piece home and completing it there. Afterwards, they would meet again and put their pieces together, thus finishing the figure in as perfect a manner as one alone had made the whole.

The richest things brought to market were of gold and silver, some of them cast, and others wrought with stones, to such perfection that many of them have surprised the ablest goldsmiths to this day, for they could never perceive how they had been made, there being no sign of hammer, or an engraver, or any other instrument used by them, the Aztecs having none such. Indeed, there were figures or representations of their kings and of their idols so perfect, so exact, that they exceeded the Spanish paintings.

It was said that in Michoacán they made images of saints, vestments, mitres, the words of consecration, and such like things so curiously, of such value, that they were sometimes worth more than if they were of gold; such nice things have been sent to the pope, that no painting can outdo them. From feathers they would make a beast, a tree, a bird, or any other thing so natural that it seemed to exceed art itself.

The artists who employed themselves in feather and gold work were legendary for having absorbed themselves so thoroughly in what they were doing, that they did not think of eating at all during the day, observing the sun, the shade, the reflection, to see whether it fit best with the grain or against it. In short, they never gave over until they had brought their creations to perfection, succeeding by sheer reason of their unwearied patience.

Each guild was to be found in a particular section of the city set aside for it, or in some community outside of the city, with its own protecting divinity and individual festivals. No one could enter into the guild except by right of descent or with the special permission of the tribal chiefs.

Imitation was the basis of instruction, even during the childhood of the Aztec boy, for in his play, he was permitted, even in his earliest days, to play with his father's trade instruments, or smaller replicas of them. This would seem to be a conscious utilization of the play impulses of the child with vocational training in mind. What is certain however, is that training in the industrial arts was acquired when the youth came of age, through an apprenticeship method.

The nature of the training, implements, skills, techniques, and methods used, and the length of the period of apprenticeship varied with the different occupations. One common factor in all vocational training, however, was learning the particular religious ritual which accompanied each type of work. Of course, too, while each member of the tribe had a field of specialization, he usually possessed a rudimentary working knowledge of many crafts.

In general, it was the custom for the sons to follow in the footsteps of their fathers, learning their trades and adopting their professions. This fact was even symbolized by the act of placing at the baptism rites the instruments of the parent's calling in the hands of the newborn baby.

A good cross-section of the many vocations which the fathers followed, and which were open to the youth, can be found in Torquemada, when he writes of the stone cutters who worked stone into almost anything; carpenters; gold and silver-smiths; painters who portrayed natural objects, especially birds, animals, trees, flowers, and such like, which they used to paint in the apartments of the kings and lords; sculptors in wood, potters, manufacturers of gourd-vessels, weavers who wove robes and garments, especially such as were worn by kings, lords, and priests, and used for the adornment and in the service of the idols; mat weavers; leather tanners; shoe makers for lords and principle men, feather workers, and obsidian knife-makers.

Bernal Diaz del Castillo mentions dancers and clowns who were in the employ of the powerful Montezuma, some dancing on stilts, tumbled, and performed a variety of other antics for the monarchs. A whole portion of the city was inhabited by these performers, and their only occupation consisted of these performances. Lastly, Montezuma had in his service great numbers of stone-cutters, masons, and carpenters solely employed in the royal palaces.

Many children were raised from childhood for the business of carrying burdens, and remained at it all their lives, and found the greater share of their work in the employ of the traveling merchants, to transport goods.

The average load for a man was fifty or sixty pounds. Some combined this task with the selling of charcoal, which they brought down from the mountains. Numerous fishermen and people of the waterfront derived their livelihood from that element, with the aid of their fishing nets and their minacachelli, which was like a harpoon with three points in a triangle, like a trident.

Those who followed the profession of medicine instructed their sons in the nature and differences of diseases, and of the herbs. The ancient Mexicans were not lacking in the tonsorial art, either, for Cortes makes mention in his Letters, of barber shops and baths. He also states that it was not an unusual sight to see in all the markets and public places many laborers and persons of various employments waiting for someone to hire them.

In the Codex Mendoza, and in the Mappe Tlotzin are pictorial representations of artisans engaged in various crafts, such as weavers, carpenters, stone carvers, lapidaries, goldsmiths and feather-mosaic workers. There are also illustrations of a carpenter teaching the craft to his son. The father is represented in the act of hewing a small tree trunk with an implement, presumably of copper.

The text of the interpreter accompanying the drawing reads, "The trades of a carpenter, jeweler (lapidary), painter, goldsmith, and embroiderer of feathers, accordingly as they are represented and declared, signify that the masters of such arts taught these trades to their sons from their earliest boyhood, in order that when grown up to be men, they might attend to their trades and spend their time virtuously, counseling them that idleness is the root and mother of vices, as well as of evil-speaking and tale-bearing, whence followed drunkenness and robberies, and other dangerous vices, and setting before their imaginations many other grounds of alarm, that hence they might submit to be diligent in everything."

The early chroniclers, in unanimity, testify to the skill and ability of the Aztec architects and builders. Motolinia records that, "There never have been or heard of before such temples as those of this land of Anahuac or New Spain, neither for size and design nor for anything else; as they rise to a great height they must needs have strong foundations; and there was an endless number of such temples and altars in this county, about which a note is here made so that those who may come to this country from now onwards may know about them, for the memory of them all has already almost perished."

"I do not wish to begin by relating the accounts given me by the Indians, but that obtained by a monk who was among the first of the conquerors who entered the country, named Fray Francisco de Aguilar, a very venerable person and one of great authority in the order of our glorious father Santa Domingo, and from other conquerors of strict veracity and authority who assured me that on the day when they entered the city of Mexico and beheld the height and beauty of the temples, they believed them to be turreted fortresses for the defense and ornament of the city, or that they were palaces and royal houses with many towers and galleries, such was their beauty and height which could be seen from afar off.

"It was indeed a most beautiful sight, for some were more lofty than the others, and some more ornamental than others, some with an entrance to the East, others to the West, others to the North, and others to the South, all plastered and sculptured, and turreted with various kinds of battlements painted with animals and figures and fortified with huge and wide buttresses of stone, and it beautified the city so greatly and gave it such an appearance of splendor that one could do nothing but stare at it."

It is indeed a great misfortune that very little remains of these numerous impressive temples, royal houses, and rich dwellings which made up the Aztec city of Mexico, and which had been constructed over many years with numberless difficulties. The Spanish Conquistadors, and nature, did a thorough job in the destruction of buildings, and the razing of the pyramids to the ground.

As a consequence, up until recent history, little was known of later Mexican architecture except what was gleaned from the accounts of the early historians. Even with the added interpretations of the findings of the newly discovered excavations, our fund of information is still far from being complete.

The original codices which have survived, are concerned mostly with religious matter, while, it can be said of the archaeological excavations, the whole region has been little more than scratched on its surface.

What has remained, however, will ever be a mystery to the greatest architects, how such small stones used in their constructions were adjusted without a single handful of mortar, and how, without sophisticated tools, merely with hard stones and sand, the Aztecs could have worked with such skill that although all this work is very old, and it is not known who did it, it has lasted until our time.

The ancient Aztecs seem to have congregated into large areas, mapped out in keeping with a fixed plan or design, to be under a central government, and in which there gradually sprang up temples, palaces, fortifications, canals, bridges, markets, public fountains, gardens, and many other carefully worked out architectural specimens.

The concrete evidences that have been unearthed do verify that the cities at their beginning were laid out after a fixed order. This would also seem to indicate that they did not owe their character or shape to accidental circumstances, or even to the site on which they were based.

The uniformity of the Mexican architecture is very instructive on this account in that it shows that it was borrowed from an older people, rather than introduced by a savage race. In the construction of edifices made of hewn stone, the ancient Aztec architects, as well as those of all Mexico and Central America, were handicapped by certain limitations, principally, the deficiency of iron tools, and the unawareness of the properties of the true arch.

The civilization of the ancient Aztecs was, from out present point of view, for all useful purposes, unaware of iron. It simply was not known to them. They possessed sufficient gold, but gold is not of much use as a material for tools. They mined copper also, but with an alloy of tin, which transformed the copper into a low-grade bronze. Then too, copper was rather scarce, and was used a great deal for ornamental reasons, and the copper-bronze axes that were made, were used for other purposes.

For the digging of the stone from the quarry, and the shaping of the stones to be used as building material, the ancient Mexicans had to depend upon stone implements, since, as a matter of fact, it is easier to quarry and carve stones than with bronze tools. One of the methods described in the treatment of stone involved, first, the leveling off of the top, and the resolving of the size of the block or blocks.

After this began, the work of hewing the sides and ends took place. It would appear that one workman sat beside the other and worked at the stone with another stone shaped like a pick, and thus the shallow furrows or low ridges were left.

The work in general resembled closely the soapstone mines of the United States, where channeling and undermining, though on a less extensive scale, were also employed.

As was mentioned above, the second handicap which limited the Aztec architects was the fact that the principles of the true arch were unknown to them. As a result of this the form of their edifices, pyramids and buildings was affected by construction in certain directions. Instead of the true arch, they used a graded stone which gave the impression of a false arch.

Some of the early chroniclers wrote of the existence of arches, but a partial explanation for this lies in their lack of knowledge concerning the real construction of this architectural element, mistaking it for the true arch which was to be found in Europe. Their only methods of roofing were by means of beams or by means of the false arch.

A chief and common characteristic of Aztec construction was the practice of erecting pyramided structures upon which they elevated a temple, an altar, or perhaps only an image of one of their gods. These pyramided substructures of the Aztecs, are unlike those to be found in Egypt with respect to form and function.

They are not carried up to a pointed apex, but terminate in a platform upon which a building in stone or wood was erected. The Egyptian pyramid was itself the building, a tomb. The American pyramid was an accessory—a platform on which to erect a building or an altar.

It is very likely that the motives which led to the construction of these immense structures were prompted by the feelings of sacredness and isolation which they seem to lend to the shrines set upon them, and also to the fact that religion was closely united with astronomy, and that a great of use was made of the temples as observatories for examination of the heavenly bodies.

Before examining some of the few existing examples of Aztec architecture which were not destroyed by the Spaniards, and which have been unearthed, let us turn to the descriptions of the Great Temple in Tenochtitlan, which furnish us with enough helpful details to realize the type of building these early New World architects constructed.

We know that an enormous wall encircled the center of the city, and that within the wall there were as many as seventy-two magnificent temples set apart for solemn devotion to the different deities of the Aztec people. From the foot of the Great Temple there stretched out in the direction of the four cardinal points, four broad paved causeways which acted as the dividing mark for the four large quarters of Tenochtitlan.

Upon reaching the valley of Mexico, after their supposedly long peregrination, the Aztecs had conceived their first duty to be the erection of a temple to their tribal god, Huitzilopochtli, on the very spot, as their tradition relates, where they had seen an eagle on a prickly pear, which was the sign for them to make their new homes there.

It was not much of a temple that they built, their first one, perhaps as early as the year 1100, but years later when they were in the military ascendancy during the rule of the tribal chieftain Ahuitzol, they set up a truly majestic temple, one befitting their beloved and greatly revered deity.

An immense wall, ten feet high and very thick, turned towards the four cardinal points, and formed the court of this Great Temple. The wall, made of stone, was overspread with a polished leveler and was decorated with carved heads of monstrous serpents, which caused it to be known as "coatepantli," or "wall of serpents."

Their decorations were ordinarily diversified and profuse, and the plumed serpent motif, which partly covered the front of a building, or placed in a line as on the coatepantli, was among the most prominent. They also had recourse to cones of stone as a part of their decorations, and which have been pointed out as architectural "bosses," or knobs.

An arsenal or storehouse for their military weapons, two stories in height, was situated in the center of each wall. These buildings were also turned in the direction of the four cardinal points. Their lower floors made up the huge doors which formed the entrance to the court of the temple. Near the center of the court was the Great Temple, consisting of a pyramid of about three hundred seventy-five feet long, by three hundred thirty-five feet wide at the base.

Their method of constructing a pyramid consisted of piling up a thick mass of stone and clay for the core of the structure, which was covered with a hard smooth layer of square stones of tezontle held fast with cement, then revested, or covered, with a coat of well-polished lime, to show a very bright exterior upon which they painted many colors, also adding carved stones to complete the picture.

From the neighboring regions, and also, frequently from afar, they obtained the necessary materials. Among the stones found to be used mostly for building purposes were granite, basalt, porphyry and tezontl, a porous type of building stone, and also adobe and brick.

The pyramid of the Great Temple rose in five stories or perpendicular terraces, with rather steep inclinations, to a height of almost thirty meters. Each one of the stories or terraces was placed about two meters away from the edge of the one immediately below, forming, in this way, a wide border.

In the center of each of the terraces was constructed a section of a stairway, whose steps measured 27 cm. in height, placed alternately on each side of the body of the pyramid so that in order to ascent the following one, it was necessary to go all the way around the edifice, thus causing an astonishing effect during the religious ceremonies, when the priests, richly dressed, ascended slowly and majestically on all sides of the pyramid. At the same time, this arrangement offered greater difficulties to attacking forces in case of war.

Above the eastern extremities there were two towers of three stories, sixteen meters high, placed at distances from the edge of the platform, scarcely sufficient to permit the passing of a man. The lower floor of the tower was of lime and stone, while the two upper ones were of wood, with the peculiarity of having windows, which could only be reached by ladder.

A wooden cupola, well-painted and profusely decorated, formed the roof of this construction.

The real sanctuaries were on the first floor; the one to the right dedicated to Huitzilopochtli, and the one across, to Tezcatlipoca. Here could be found gigantic statues, representing those deities, hidden from the view of the multitudes by rich curtains, embroidered in the lower parts with small golden cascabels, which produced light sounds when the curtains moved.

In front of the chapels was the sacrificial stone, in view of the people. The walls and ceilings of the sanctuary were covered with paintings, representative of monstrous figures, ornamented with stucco and precious woods, and here, the walls as well as the roof were spattered with human blood, from which emanated a thick, ferocious odor.

The upper floors served as a deposit for the ashes of dead kings, and for the keeping of the diverse instruments necessary for use in the temple.

In front of each one of the towers or chapels was placed a huge brasero, upon which was constantly burning the sacred fire, watched over by the priests and virgins, who kept it always alive, for its extinction would produce terrible calamities. Also here was the pan-huehuetl, or drum, whose deep vibrating resonance could be heard by all from great distances.

The most magnificent monuments of all Aztec architecture which were to be found in their capital city of Tenochtitlan, were lost to the world, when the death struggle with the Conquistadors terminated in the destruction of the entire city.

The task of the archaeologist endeavoring to ascertain the truth of the early writings concerning these architectural splendors, was beset with great difficulty, for it seemed as though nothing of importance had been saved for posterity.

From time to time, however, some remains are unearthed, which make possible the valid determination of the chief constructive features of Aztec architecture, as for example, the temple brought to light at the corner of Guatemala and Argentine streets in the Federal District of Mexico, and a stairway that may be observed in the cellars of the Secretariat of Industry.

As yet, there has not been discovered within Mexico City proper a building with all its parts intact, that would disclose to examination its structural arrangement, quality of walls, design of the rooms, appearance of floors, and the state of the stairways, so completely did the Spaniards carry out their self-imposed task of destruction.

In order to estimate justly the architectural accomplishments of the Aztecs at the time of the conquest, we find it necessary to go outside of the City of Mexico to some remains found at Santa Cecilia, a place near Tenayucan, in Teopanzalco near Cuernavaca, and Tepozteco, very close to the village of tepoztlan, Morelos.

Of these comparatively recent excavations, Mexican archaeologists consider the pyramid at the village of Tenayucan, which is about six miles northeast of Mexico City, to be one of the most notable examples of Aztec architecture.

Over five centuries ago, the Aztecs, in a fit of frenzy and fear, attempted to conceal this pyramid from the conquering Spaniards, with a covering of earth. In this manner, the pyramid remained throughout the years, but not untouched, for the natives of the nearby villages were aware of its existence, and took from it stones when needed with almost the feeling that some divine foresight had placed a quarry there for their benefit, with blocks of uniform size.

With the covering removed, and brought back to its former state as much as possible, the pyramid, which is now exposed to view, is of earth and rock, faced with cut stone and plaster. It is square and about sixty feet high. Serpents carved of stone stick their heads out of the slanting pyramid walls, like peering sentinels.

Around three sides of the pyramid, near its base, is lined a whole regiment of these guardian snakes, one hundred thirty eight of them. Flecks of red, blue and green paint still cling to the heads and bodies of the serpents. On the front of the pyramid rises a grand stairway, carved with hieroglyphics.

The shrine for which this pyramid was the substructure, has completely disappeared.

The conclusions which Mexican archaeologists present with respect to the chief characteristics of the ancient Aztec architecture, after examination of the above excavation, and similar ones at Santa Cecilia and Teopanzolco, are as follows: walls of slight grade, with taluses or slopes of steep inclinations, decorated by bosses or knobs made up of carved serpents, and interrupted by narrow spaces not intended for use as passageways; low masonry partitions dividing the stairways up these pyramids; the central coping by change of slope furnishing small landing-stages or platforms.

Later structures, sometimes two or even more, were very often placed upon or superimposed on the earlier. At Tenayucan, in particular, these Mexican archaeologists distinguished four clear epochs of construction.

Another type of architecture to be found in Aztec construction, was the round temple, surmounted by a high, peaked, thatched roof. These were erected by the ancient Mexicans to their god Quetzalcoatl. Torquemada declared, "These Indians of New Spain built their temples to the God of the Air, of a circular shape, because, as air circulates and surrounds all, his temple had to manifest his qualities.

"The entrance to such a temple had the shape and figure of the mouth of a fierce great serpent, represented in the way our painters depict the mouth of hell with its horrible frightful eyes, teeth and fangs. The roof of the famous temple, and of others that surround it, were of different and various shapes, although some were of wood and others thatched with a straw resembling rye-straw."

The rarity of these round temples among Mexican ruins can be explained by the fact that the thatched roofs of the temples made them capable of being easily set on fire, thus facilitating their destruction by the Spaniards who desired to erase from sight immediately such pagan monstrosities as the temples with the serpent-jawed doorways.

An important discovery of a round temple was made in 1930 at Calixtlahuaca, some forty miles west of Mexico city; and in 2007, archaeologists have discovered the ruins of an 800-year-old Aztec pyramid in the central Tlatelolco area, once a center for the Aztec elite. The ruins are about 36 feet high, and may have been built as early as the year 1100, suggesting that the Aztecs began to develop their civilization in central Mexico much earlier than previously believed.

The dwelling places of the chieftains and nobles were both spacious and massive, built of stone and lime, sometimes clay, and erected on terraces or platforms, the lowest of which was six feet high, the highest, thirty to forty feet in height long and as many wide.

The buildings ordinarily surrounded a court, directly off which were to be found the rooms which they required; the sleeping quarters and reception rooms for the men in one section, and those of the women in another; their storerooms, kitchens and corrals in another still.

It was also customary to have a garden alongside of the court where the girls and young women of the family could move about under the watchful eye of the governesses.

Frequently, these dwellings had upper stories, and the roofs of the most important had level surfaces and were battlemented. One of the original Conquistadors described them as being very well built, of beautiful stone work and cedar wood, and the wood of other sweet-scented trees; with great rooms and courts, wonderful to behold, covered with awnings of cotton cloth.

The Aztecs had also perfected the use of stucco as an exterior covering to masonry so excellently during their time, that from a distance it seemed like silver to the first of the Spanish invaders. Bernal Diaz mentions that occurrence which took place upon Cortes' arrival at the Totonac town of Capoala.

He writes, "Our scouts who were on horseback, reached a great plaza with courts, where they had prepared our quarters, and it seems that during the last few days they had been whitewashed and burnished, a thing they knew well how to do, and it seemed to one of the scouts that this white surface which shone so brightly must be of silver, and he came back at full speed to tell Cortes that the walls of the houses were made of silver."

Concerning the domestic architecture of the houses of the masses, very little is known yet. Throughout the Valley of Mexico, and even southward, the houses of the humbler people, consisting of only one room, were simply constructed with walls made of adobe (sun-dried mud), sometimes stone, wood or reeds, and with flat wooden or thatched roofs, while those with more wealth usually possessed an ajauhcalli, or orator, and a temazcalli or steam bath.

The amount of labor involved in all the heavy construction work done by the ancient Mexicans must have been tremendous. But labor, as has already been expressed, from one point of view, is a matter of time, and time does not hold much value for primitive peoples, and neither time nor labor were regarded as important hindrances to the erection of enormous architectural complexes by the early American architects.

The heavy labor, most likely, was shifted to the slaves and subject peoples, and captives.

The construction of a gigantic structure like a pyramid or public building, however, would require a division of specialized labor and workers, each of whom needed special and separate training.

Therefore, we see that there were also available to the Aztec youths such occupations as temple artisans, porters, engineers, decorators, painters, sculptors, engravers, casters, stone cutters, carpenters, and of course, architects.

It seems that the crafts which called for creativeness and skill and a long period of apprenticeship, were more highly regarded by the Aztecs than the simple jobs of labor. Whereas the laborers were paid in food and clothing, the skilled artisans received in addition, gold, chocolate, and painted cloths.

We are able to distinguish the various skilled occupations which resulted from the many uses made of the abundance of wood obtained by the Aztecs from the neighboring forests and the mountains and slopes surrounding the Valley of Mexico.

In these places, as well as certain sections of the Valley itself, there were large trees of unusually high qualities of hard and soft wood, which were found to be easily converted to suit the needs of the ancient Mexicans.

First of the callings connected with timber and wood that can be singled out are the foresters or lumbermen who, by means of their copper hatchets and well-sharpened axes, cut down the trees, hewing them smoothly and cleaning away the chips, to facilitate their transport.

Before actually setting about the work of felling the trees, however, the forester, in keeping with his religious and superstitious beliefs, would make some offerings and prayers to the guardian spirits of the forests. This, plus some other superstitious actions, was a part of the religious training which the apprentices had had to absorb alongside of his actual instruction in workmanship.

The Aztecs adored as gods certain trees, such as the cypress, cedar and oak, before which they made their sacrifices; indeed, at home, they planted them in an orderly fashion around their fountains.

Continuing with the description of the nature of their work, there was no lack of plants from which the Aztecs made string, cords and cables, as though from hemp. Boring a hole through one side of the beam, they passed a cable to which slaves were harnessed, as though they were oxen under the yoke. Instead of wheels, they placed rounded tree-trunks on the road, whether going up or down hill.

The carpenters oversaw the work, but the slaves did the heaviest part of it. All materials and whatever was required in daily life was carried in the same way, for they had neither oxen nor any other animals as beasts of burden.

Incredible stories were told of these pieces of wood. Numerous eye-witnesses wrote about them, at length. One of these beams, found at Tezcuco was one hundred and twenty feet long, and thick and around as a fat ox. It sustained almost an entire building.

Exceedingly large quantities of wood of several varieties, cypress, cedar, oak, laurel, spruce, pine and other kinds common to tropical and semi-tropical regions, were needed by the ancient Aztecs for many special purposes other than serving as a material for fuel or timber for buildings, and this wood, gathered from the neighboring dense forests or through tribute, was placed on sale, daily, in the great market of Tlaltelolco, both in the rough, or manufactured in various ways.

There were other trees which they called olquavitl; they were large and high, and contained much liquid. From these trees there was secreted a black resin called ulli, which was medicinal for the eyes, for abscesses and tumors and putrefactions, and the bowels when they were closed.

The ancient Aztecs carpenters capitalized to the fullest degree upon the plentiful supply of timber that was available, and over the course of years, erected houses, and filled in the swamps surrounding the lakes of the valley, with millions of stakes and planks.

It is interesting to note that in the year 1900, when excavations were conducted on the site of old Tenochtitlan in the city of Mexico, in connection with the laying of pipes for an improved system of drainage in the present Avenida de Guatemala, back of the Cathedral, many thousands of stakes were discovered, about fifteen feet below the present level of the city, driven there when new land was needed by the ancient Mexicans for the building of the Aztec capital. Parts of earthenware water pipes in which crystalline water was still flowing, were found at the time, to the astonishment of witnesses.

Then too, as Tenochtitlan was a city intersected with numerous canals and parallel paved roads, and crossed by many bridges, through which canals innumerable canoes plied their way from neighboring settlements on the lake shores, one may judge of the enormous quantity of wood used along the sides of the canals, in the construction of bridges, and for the fabrication of the canoes themselves.

While the smaller vessels may have been constructed for personal use by individuals, large canoes having a capacity for carrying a number of persons and rowers, especially for state and other festive occasions, were made by the carpenters, as were skiffs capacious enough to hold from one to five people, not forgetting the oars for all.

We know that canoe traffic in Tenochtitlan was considerable, and so this part of the carpenter's trade must have been a busy one. Adding to the picture of the city, canoes paddled the water all through the streets, and men were stationed on the top who were paid to fill them where the conduits cross.

At the different entrances to the city, and wherever the canoes were unloaded, which was where the greatest quantity of provisions entered the city, there were guards in huts to collect a certain tariff of everything that entered. Further, all the streets had openings at regular intervals to let the water flow from one to the other, and at all of these openings, some which were very broad, there were bridges, large, strong and well constructed, so that over many of them ten or more horsemen could ride abreast.

In addition also, to the dwellings of the well-to-do and chieftains, and the religious temples and pyramids erected by the carpenter, there was to be found alongside of this particular type of construction the work of the wood-carver, whose few examples which have not been destroyed or lost, reveal a great deal of skill and proficiency.

These craftsmen, carved and painted or gilded great quantities of wood in order to produce for the interior of both house and temple, ceiling sheathings, finished household idols, pieces of furniture, such as tables, chairs, screens, chests, wardrobes, and also ceremonial objects and wooden vessels and jars, all of a wondrous beauty.

Their highly ornate designs were engraved with a delicacy not excelled by the work of any other people of antiquity, and certainly equal to the best carved wood of ancient Egypt.

We find words of praise of their workmanship also in Cortes' description of the many temples of their capital city. He writes, "They are so well built, in both their masonry and their woodwork, that they could not be better made or constructed anywhere; for all the masonry inside the chapels, where they keep their idols, are carved with figures, and the woodwork is all wrought with designs of monsters and other shapes."

Woodcarving, beautifully executed, was also to be found among their wooden weapons of warfare. These latter included bows fashioned of easily bent wood, some of which were so long that their strings came to as much as five feet in length; wooden helmets and shields; quauhololli the maquahuitl, a weapon often used by the Aztecs to bring disaster to their enemies, and referred to as a kind of saw-sword made of wood, with double-edged rows of inserted razor-like obsidian knives; and their atlatl or spear-thrower, described as being ornamented with finely and skillfully executed carvings in low-relief of human figures and symbols.

They cover both sides of the atlatl and extend from its upper end to the end of the grooves. Sometimes, over the whole surface of the carefully carved atlatl, there was spread a fine layer of the purest gold, to which was still further added an inlay of turquoise and a flat covering of feathers.

The wood carver's art was also put to excellent use in the manufacture of wooden covers for their books of codices, that is, for the ones deemed of considerable importance, since most had only a thick, stiff skin cover. Intricate carvings were also to be found on the wooden drums huehuetl and teponaztli, wooden masks, the many wooden idols, representing many of the principal deities of the Mexicans, and gilded wooden frames in which were set mirrors of highly polished slabs of obsidian, of rectangular, square, or circular shapes, all exhibiting the remarkable degree of skill attained by an industrious and intelligent race, a fitting epitome of the strange civilization of ancient Mexico, their real barbarism tempered by the most marvelous perfection in every detail of their industrial arts.

We find many descriptions of the different uses of mosaic work in ancient Mexico. The major employment of the mosaic art was in the embellishment of such objects or ornaments as crowns or head bands, ear-ornaments, nose ornaments, breast plates, bracelets and anklets.

While wood was the chief material on which the mosaic covering was usually placed, gold, shell, bone, and stone were also used. Some of their musical instruments, as well as small figures of the gods, either in human or animal form were similarly decorated. Even pottery vessels were embellished by means of embedding turquoise in the clay.

Bearing a general likeness to the art of the mosaic-worker in stone, was that of the mosaic-worker in feathers. As with other trades in Aztec times requiring artistic manual ability, the art of mosaic-work in feathers was in the hands of a special "guild" made up of families tracing their origins to the earliest nomadic immigrants from the north into the Valley of Mexico.

It is indeed tragic that the only knowledge we possess of these wonderful masterpieces of Mexican craftsmanship has been culled almost entirely from the ancient codices and the recordings of the early chroniclers because of the fact that the nature of the materials used made them extremely susceptible to decay. Scarcely a single specimen has been preserved for us down to the present time, and that only in a sorrowfully mutilated condition.

The Aztecs produced their feather-works in two very different ways. By one method, they arranged the feathers on a framework, stringing and tying them together by means of thread and twine. By the other method, their artisans pasted them on thin cotton paper.

The first method was used in making devices which the Mexican chiefs and warriors wore in war and on the occasion of religious dances. By the other method they made the feather cloaks which served to adorn the idols and plates forming the outside of their shields. This last method was undoubtedly the one which demanded the most skill and most highly refined artistic taste.

That which is especially to be noted is the fact that they knew how to heighten the effect of the colors of the feathers by the same process our artists employ today, i.e., that they superimposed the layers in spectacularly intricate fashion.

They paid attention at the same time, to economy, using for the under layer only the common feathers, but having the color of these harmonize brilliantly with that of the costly feathers spread above.

The highly technical and involved skill of the methods of the ancient native handwork of the feather-workers may be observed further through a description of the still-surviving "Vienna feather-piece" which one Herr Von Hochstetter preserved for his private collection.

The fan-shaped base of this feather-piece is composed of harmoniously disposed concentric bands of delicate feather-work studded with thin-beaded golden plates of different shapes, provided with small asymmetrical perforations by means of which they were stitched in place.

The crescent-shaped gold ornaments and the smaller tile-shaped ones exhibit, moreover, small projections, evidently meant to be concealed, on which these holes were pierced with uncanny unanimity.

Next to the magnificent loose fringe, which was originally composed of about five hundred of the long tail feathers, of which each male quetzal bird possesses but two, the most striking and beautiful feature of the specimen is the broad turquoise blue band.

On this a design is uniformly executed with the diminutive tile-shaped gold pieces of which were counted no less than fourteen hundred. Overlapping each other, like fish scales, these are so disposed as to form a flexible, rectilinear pattern architectonic in outline and somewhat resembling a series of small towers.

The back of the object resembles somewhat, an open, modern fan, and is composed of a firm, net-like fabric, woven with incredible accuracy, of finely twisted agave fibers, stiffened by twenty eight thin sticks covered with fibre and woven into the net at regular intervals.

The quills of the feathers are so skillfully knotted to this net that the front, with its series of sharply defined symmetrical concentric bands forms a closely covered, flexible texture, corresponding exactly on both sides, the radial width of the network and its concentric bands being exactly 28.5 cm.

This confirms the accounts given by the early Spaniards of the truly admirable skill of Mexican industrial art in all its branches. The structural detail of just this one masterpiece makes us realize the immense amount of experience that must have preceded its manufacture, and marvel at the foresight and care with which it is executed.

Among the occupations for women were spinning and weaving, embroidering and lace work at which they were remarkably clever. There was an allied trade of makers of rush mats, "petates," and those who weaved seats for stools, called, "icpales."

They worshiped the god Napatecutli, for it was believed that he was the god who invented the art of making mats, and by his grace that reed and rush were planted and grew, thus making it possible for them to work at their trade.

Exceptional ability in these arts was an accomplishment which formed an essential part of every girl's education, from the highest to the lowest. Weaving and embroidery were regarded as arts of such importance by the ancient Mexicans that they were placed under the protection of a special goddess, Xochiquetzal.

Among the other occupations that seemed to be open to women and girls was the manufacture of salt.

Salt ranked next to chili in importance as the condiment most frequently used. Since the valley of Mexico was the source of most of the supply of salt, a good subsistence should have been derived from the manufacture of it. We know, however, that the state obtained a considerable income from the duties imposed upon the traffic of the article, and that, in addition, since the Aztecs practically monopolized the market, only those tribes from whom they exacted tribute could purchase salt.

Of the primitive methods used by the Aztecs to obtain salt, the best quality was obtained by boiling the water from the salt lake in large pots, preserving it in large white cakes. Most frequently, however, the water was led by trenches into shallow pools and there left to be evaporated by the sun.

A poorer quality of salt was used mostly for salting and preserving meats. Brick-colored, and strongly saturated, it was obtained by being scraped up on the flats around the lakes.

The manufacture of paper became increasingly important to the Aztecs, as their influence grew in the region. The reasons for this will be enumerated in the following discussion. The process employed in paper production began with the macerating of the leaves of various plants, such as agave, until the fleshy parts became separated.

The filaments were then cleaned and distributed into layers which were made smooth and formed into sheets. Examination of these sheets reveals that some resinous substance, for example, gypsum or lime, prepared as a paste, was applied to both surfaces.

Strong pressure was then exerted upon both sides of the paper after each had been covered with a thin membrane, probably deerskin, until the sheet gave the impression of being made up of the substance of the dressing itself. As a result of this smoothly polished surface supplied by the membrane, the painters were enabled to draw and paint as neatly and effectively as they did.

In addition to whatever paper was manufactured by the Aztecs themselves, a large amount in the many thousands of sheets, was received by them yearly as tribute, which fact leads us to ask, just what use did they make of all that paper, since the number of people trained in the art of hieroglyphic painting was small.

The recording of the historical annals of the year, which was usually confined to the most important civic, religious and military occurrences; the registering of tributes; drafting of maps for varied purposes such as in a case of litigation concerning the limits of rural estates for the enlightenment of the judges; literary pursuits; priestly recordings of the ritual calendar, and other similar activities, could not have exhausted within a year all that paper.

Further investigation into the methods of disposal of the remainder brings us to the religious festivals, ritual and official paper cutters.

Paper was employed in all the festivals held during each of the eighteen months of the year, for the dressing up of the temples, idols, victims, priests, trees, and even all of those persons who participated in the ceremonies, or simply observed them.

Here we are making reference only to the monthly festivals held during the Mexican ritual calendar. Every day was, so to speak, sanctified, having its special patron, before whose shrine it was the priest's duty to offer sacrifice, by burning balls of copal, hule, and amatl (resin, rubber and paper).

If we now consider that the copantli (wall of serpents, which formed the large enclosure in the midst of which arose the structure of the famous pyramid) was studded with seventy-eight such shrines and oratories, each of which was to be attended daily, we may form an idea of the enormous quantity of paper that was consumed in the special department of worship alone.

The festival of the tenth month called Xocotlvetzi called for the official paper cutters who adorned the trees used in the festival with papers placed on them with much care. A statue resembling a man and made of a dough of wild amaranth seeds was also adorned with papers. The paper used was pure white, without paint or dye.

On the head of this statue they fastened cut papers which looked like hair; on both sides they fastened paper stoles reaching from the right shoulder to the left armpit. On the arms they put paper fashioned like waves on which were figures of the sparrow-hawk.; He also received a belt of paper. Above this, other papers placed back and front simulated the vipil, or blouse and shirt.

On the sides of the statue and on the tree, from the feet of the former down to about the middle of the tree, long papers were hung, which waved in the air. These latter were about three feet long.

Paper served as easily prepared images of the gods to which they were offered, usually with a representation of the god, picture or symbol, drawn on the paper with liquid caoutchouc, one of the most common sacrificial gifts, especially to the rain-gods.

A considerable amount of paper material was used to complement the Aztec dress, to heighten their appearance, especially so at their religious performances and ceremonies.

We also know that paper was placed on sale in the market place, which fact permits us to assume that much was bought for family use, for the dress of both the women and men, for their headgear, etc., and also for their daily religious offerings, and for the occasional burial ritual.

We may recall that out of the many laws and prescribed practices of the ancient Mexicans, mention was made of one that was intended to regulate the sales and transactions of numerous kinds of articles or objects of speculative value on particular set days and market fairs.

We know that there were two great slave markets, Atzcapotzalco and Izucar. The market for jewels was at Cholula, and fine earthenware, feather work, gourd cups, garments, and precious stones were obtainable at Tezcuco. The thickly inhabited city of Acolman, ranking second in importance in the kingdom, was renowned as the principle and only dog market.

The raising of dogs was a most highly profitable business as well as being one of singular importance. It was believed by the Aztec people that if anyone born under the sign "nauictzcuintli" devoted himself to the occupation of breeding little dogs, any amount that he wished to raise would multiply and give him pleasure, and he would become wealthy through them, because they were in such great demand.

It was customary among the Aztecs to eat the meat of small castrated dogs, and as a result of its tastiness, it occupied a conspicuous place in the diet of the ancient Mexicans. As evidence of its savoriness, we can point to the fact that the Spaniards took to the dog meat so favorably that in a short while after the conquest, the supply was depleted.

It seems, however, that dogs were desired by the natives not only for their use as a food, and for their loyalty and devotion, and for their symbolic role in weddings and baptisms, but for the most part, because of the unusual role of the animal in what the Aztecs believed was the "region beyond death." This will be explained in a short while.

Three types of dogs which were raised by the breeders are referred to: the "xoloitzcuintli," which was used as a pack animal for light burdens, as a watchdog, and as a protector on trips and short strolls; the "itzcuintepotzolli," considerably smaller than the former, raised to grace eventually the tables of the well-to-do as a food; and red colored dogs, also of this class, for the purpose of serving as sacrificial offerings at the funeral rites of the dead.

The third species of dog was the "tepeitzccuiantli," or mountain dog, which was the size of a small cub, and as ferocious as a hyena. This dog was fearless, frequently attacking deer and often killing them. It seems that none of these native dogs knew how to bark, and usually expressed their different emotions of anger, content, and annoyance, through a howling process. It is said that they did eventually learn how to bark from those dogs which were introduced into Mexico by the Spanish.

These three distinct types of canine, each having its own peculiar function to fulfill, predicate some knowledge of breeding which had to be passed on from father to son in the latter's apprenticeship, including instructions in proper methods of propagating the dogs, and their later training.

Indicative of other skills and functions to be mastered, we find that the dogs destined to be eaten, were wrapped in cloths at night. From the time they were very young, the Aztecs rubbed their outer covering with gum oxitl (turpentine), which caused their hair to fall out.

At the time for killing the dog, it was tradition to place its head into a hole in the soil made for that purpose, and choke it. Between caresses and stroking its back, the owner would tie a loose cotton string around its neck, and recite the traditional words, much to the effect of, "Wait for me over there my friend because you have to help carry me across the nine rivers of hell."

The important role played by the dogs in the everyday life and religion of the ancient Aztecs must have placed great demands upon the breeders, such that Acolman, the second largest populated city of Tezcuco was granted the unique privilege of being the only market fair at which dogs could be purchased.

According to the beliefs of the Aztecs, the souls of the departed were immortal; they went to one of three different places when separated from the body, which latter was disposed of either by burial or cremation.

Those soldiers who died in battle or in captivity among the enemies, and those of women who died during childbirth, went to the House of the Sun, whom they considered as the Prince of Glory, where they led a life of endless delight, and where every day at the first appearance of the sun's rays they hailed the sight with rejoicing, dancing, the music of instruments and voices, attending the sun to its meridian; there they met the souls of the women, and with the same festivity, accompanied the sun to its setting.

It seems that the Aztecs, at some point in their development, very shrewdly observed the concept that if religion was intended to serve the purpose of government, as has been imagined by most of the free thinkers of our times, surely the nations could not forge a system of belief better calculated to inspire their soldiers with courage than one which promised so high a reward after their deaths.

They next supposed that these spirits, after four years of that glorious life, went to animate the clouds, and birds of beautiful feathers and sweet song; but always they were at liberty to rise again to heaven or to descend upon the earth to warble and feed upon the most fragrant flowers.

Those men who died in battle or on the altar as a sacrifice to the gods, (and in the minds of the Aztecs there was no distinction between the two, since both kinds of death were befitting a warrior), and those women who died in childbirth, were cremated.

The souls of those that were drowned, struck by lightning, or died by wounds, tumors, fevers, or other such disasters, went, as the ancient Mexicans believed, along with the souls of children, to a cool and delightful place called Tlalocan. The bodies of those who entered Tlalocan were always buried.

Lastly, the other kind of death was the Mictlan, or hell, which they conceived to be a place of utter darkness, in which reigned a god called Mictlantecutli, (Lord of Hell), and a goddess named Mictlancihuatl. They did not imagine that the souls underwent any other punishment than what they suffered from the permanent darkness of their abode.

The souls of the dead who went to hell were the souls of people who had died of some disease, be they lords, chiefs, or common people. On the day of the death, the friends and relatives would gather around the body as it lay on the bed before the burial, and make some speeches of consolation to both the deceased and the immediate kin.

At this point, the very old men and the official paper-cutters proceeded to cut, adorn and tie the papers as was their duty for the dead; they tied the legs together, dressed the body with those papers, tied the papers to it, then poured drops of water over it.

They then placed the body in the burial shroud, this being the way they buried their dead, with its blankets and papers, tying it tightly.

Often, a jewel was placed into the mouth of the corpse, because the Aztecs believed that it entered the body as a heart. If the body were to be cremated, the jewel was carefully searched for afterward, to be set aside and preserved in the burial box with a lock of the dead person's hair, and the remains of ashes and bones.

Those who perished in a distant land, as on a trading expedition, or on the battlefield, and whose mortal remains were not available to lay to rest, were also remembered in an Aztec "ceremony in memory of the dead." The obsequies held in honor for those left behind in war were always more pretentious for the purpose of publicly expressing recognition of the distinguished service rendered by the deceased.

When a chief or lord died, the Aztecs made many and diverse ornaments of paper, consisting of a banner or pennant of four fathoms in length, adorned with different plumes, and they also killed at least twenty slaves. It was thought that since in this world the slaves had attended him, so they had to continue to serve him in his next life.

It has been concluded by modern anthropologists that this dual practice of cremation and burial of the ancient Mexicans is a clear indication that the nomadic immigrant worshipers of Huitzilopochtli, who was identified with the warrior's Paradise Of The Sun, regularly burned the bodies of their dead, while the original inhabitants of the Valley, who recognized the supremacy of Tlaloc, buried their dead without reducing the bodies to ashes.

The present archaeological evidence tends to uphold this conclusion.

It is interesting to speculate about the possible Asiatic influences under which the pre-Columbian culture of America developed. In the religion of old Mexico, four great scenes in the so-called Journey Of The Soul in the land of the dead are depicted in a group in the Aztec picture-writing now known as the Vatican Codex.

The four scenes are first, the crossing of the river on its journey to hell; second, the fearful passage of the soul between two mountains which clash together; third, the soul's passage up the mountain set with sharp obsidian knives; fourth, the dangers of the wind carrying those knives on its blast.

Compare these picture-writings with some similar pictures of Buddhist origin depicting their conception of "hells," or purgatories, from Japanese temple scrolls.

In these latter, we can find first, the river of death where the souls of the dead wade across; second, the souls have to pass between two huge iron mountains which are pushed together by two demons; third, the guilty souls climb the mountain of knives, whose blades cut their hands and feet; and fourth, fierce blasts of wind drive against their lacerated forms the blades of knives flying through the air.

The appearance of analogies so complex, so close, to Buddhist ideas in Mexico, constituted a correspondence of so high an order as to preclude any explanation except the direct transmission of ideas from one religion to another.

This theory of course, is still very much subject to controversy, many questions of course remaining to be answered definitively—in the fullness of time.

9

Conclusions

It is evident that the Aztecs were passing through a transitional stage at the time of the Conquest, evolving from a loose democratic federation of clans, into something approaching a militaristic aristocracy grasping control away from the clans.

As further evidence of a developing aristocracy, official recognition of class differences appeared in 1502, when Montezuma II, after his election as tribal chieftain, ordered the dismissal from all positions of importance throughout the Aztec kingdom, all those who were not of the ruling caste.

This was a step of major importance. The Codex Ramirez relates that only a few days after Montezuma assumed his position, he set about to remove all those of "low birth" so that the kingdom should be served only by people of "good birth."

Whether or not this act of "hubris" set the stage for their later downfall, only future history will decide.

What is not in dispute, however is the fact that after the arrival of the Spanish Conquistadors, the Aztecs went into a decline from which they never recovered.

It is the opinion of the author that this can be directly traced to the Spaniards wresting control of their education away from them, and substituting their own priests for those of the natives.

No civilization as complex as that of the Aztecs could possibly have been maintained without a well-defined system of education, and this was key to all their many successes and advancements.

To think of their education, however, in a formalized sense, such as the imparting of knowledge through schools, would be to mistake a part for the whole, for schooling and education are not necessarily synonymous.

An ethnographer in the field who explores this subject in such a fashion will be attacking the problem from an inadequate and restricted viewpoint.

If we accept the whole of the environment as the instrument of man's education in the widest sense, then certain factors become more clearly apparent as being more effectively active. Of these factors, we see that school is only one.

Looking upon education then, in a broad view, as the transmission of culture, to describe the content of Aztec education would be to describe the whole life of the people.

Therefore, we can say that their whole-life "curriculum" dealt with the most intimate, primitive, and practical affairs of life—from birth to death; it dealt with the mores and customs, with eating, drinking and marrying, with worship of the gods, and the daily intercourse with one's fellow-men at work, in the house, the street, the field, the market, the temple, at drill, or on the battlefield, and at festive (and otherwise) occasions.

In the early years of a child's life at home, the parents, the family, the priests and the clan served as instructors. Some things were taught as they had to be, systematically, but much was also acquired without a sense of being schooled, through the natural processes of imitation and play, and also through active and passive participation in the many ceremonious activities, religious, economic, social and military, which made up so much of their daily life.

The training of the Aztec child was severe from its very beginning, and the pedagogical methods of the parents were strict. As a result of their historical background and their development into a war-like people, the ancient Aztecs aimed decidedly to make their children become strong, hardened, and dexterous.

All physical activities were conducted, therefore, in keeping with rigid precepts. While the children may have found time for play, games, and amusements, the universal maxim of elders seems to have been to keep the young boys and girls constantly occupied, with a careful check on their manners and morals.

In spite of the severe punishments inflicted frequently, there is ample evidence that proves that the Aztecs loved their children warmly and tenderly.

The very nature of their ceremonies centering about the home also brought about closer family ties, and helped in the maintenance of the strong family bond. The results of their method of upbringing tended to make the children respect parents, elders, fear their gods and authorities, and yield easily to social pressure.

According to the plan of education depicted in the Mendoza Codex, the Aztecs recognized distinct periods in a child's life, and modified their training and instruction accordingly.

One of the weak spots to be detected in their pedagogy is common with us today, as well: example was not deemed sufficient without precept. On the contrary, all human experience demonstrates that it is easy to implant emotional prejudices, but very hard indeed to teach useful principles which run counter to natural inclination.

The Aztecs indulged only too often in sage, long-winded, oft-repeated harangues to their offspring. Thus, amid a flood of verbiage, an Aztec father would bid his son to work industriously, be humble in social relations, emulate the examples of an eminent kinsman, practice moderation in fleshly indulgences, and follow the golden middle path in life choices, eschewing both extravagance and squalors.

The high standards of character and good morals of the Aztecs are reflected in these exhortations, proverbs, and prayers of the people.

Public opinion and the desire to conform to the existing mores also played their parts in tribal life. Their notions of morality were raised to the rank of legal precepts, setting up punishments for such acts as murder, adultery, theft, bribery, drunkenness, false practices in medicine and business, and violation of contracts.

At the first signs of maturity, the children of these ancient Mexicans could be sent to the public seminaries attached to the local temples. The education in the Calmecac, the tribal temple school for the children of the nobility and well-to-do, was in the main of a religious nature.

The priest instructors taught the reading and writing of hieroglyphics, oratory, tradition, arithmetic, chronology, history, mythology, geography, poetry, music, songs, dances, games, principles of government, tribal law, astronomy, astrology, divination, such natural history and science as were known to the Aztecs at that time, and religion. Instruction was oral but was not offered in a manner of formalized classes.

Whatever was learned was acquired as natural and necessary adjuncts to the daily life and religious ritual.

Training in the Calmecac was offered first on an elementary or intermediate level in which specialization for the priesthood, military or the more important civil careers would take place.

While there was no coeducation, seminaries for the girls and young women of the upper classes were organized with the express aim of increasing to the utmost their retiring and industrious domesticity.

There they would remain until marriage, or, if they so chose, they had the privilege of taking perpetual religious vows and remaining for life in the Calmecac and temple, in which case they were permitted to participate in the intimate services of the temple.

Since it was required of every adult member of the tribe to be prepared to respond to the call to arms, the fathers would start the actual training for warriorhood at an early stage of a boy's life. Skill in the use of weapons was acquired through hunting and fishing, when the father taught the son to use bow and arrow, dart, and javelin.

The parents of the middle classes, that is, the smaller merchants, petty chieftains, and the land-holding agricultural classes, generally delivered their children at about the age of twelve, to special priests and warriors for education in another seminary set aside for them in the local temples. We will recall that they were called Telpuchcalli, and were essentially training houses in which the "bachelors" received instruction in the profession of arms.

The elementary curriculum of the Telpuchcalli, similar to the Calmecac, embraced a practical course in arts and crafts, religious instruction, history and tradition, instruction in songs, rhythmic dancing, a rigid moral and physical training, and instruction in the use of weapons and military warfare.

Their advanced training was received in actual fighting on the battlefield.

Since the priesthood constituted the faculty for instruction in their arts and sciences, the Calmecac was also, by its very nature, the training school for future teachers. Undoubtedly, the amount of material covered in the different subjects in the Telpuchcalli did not compare with the more esoteric learning of the Calmecac.

Girls of the middle classes were made ready for married life by instruction in seminaries modeled after those of the boys. Their training was confined strictly to the domestic arts; spinning, weaving, cooking, sweeping the temples, and feather work.

The rules to be adhered to were strict, and punishments for infractions of regulations were harsh. Marriage was always encouraged by the tribe, and was often the immediate step taken after graduation ceremonies.

It is safe to conclude, from all we have observed, that a woman's position among the Aztecs was unquestionably inferior to that of the men.

Close review of our earliest sources for information concerning the opportunities for the underprivileged groups, including the landless peon and slaves to enjoy a formal schooling reveals that the great majority were in no position to take advantage of the education offered by both Calmecac and Telpuchcalli.

Although no legal barriers may have been imposed by the Aztecs, one of the customs observed, which tended to limit the entrance of students of the lower classes to the public seminaries, was that of bestowing handsome gifts upon the priests prior to a child's being admitted, and likewise, upon graduation just prior to marriage.

The only schooling for a large percentage of the Aztec youth of the lower classes was, therefore, the military training acquired in actual combat on the battlefield, in the act of offering services to the tribe.

By patiently piecing together fragments of information to be found in the surviving picture-writings and Codices, we can construct a picture of the vocational education of the Aztec youth. Imitation was recognized as the basis for this instruction.

Even during the childhood of the Aztec boys and girls, he or she was encouraged to play with the various "trade" instruments of both mother and father: the boys with their father's tools, the girls, with their mother's implements. This was a conscious utilization of the play impulses of the child, with vocational training in mind.

Training in the industrial arts of the time was acquired when the youth came of age, through an apprenticeship method. The number of occupations open to the Aztec was many and varied, ranging from the highly specialized and complex crafts with their "guild system," to the simple performances of an average worker and farmer.

The nature of the training, mastery of tools and implements, skills, techniques and methods, the ethical and professional attitudes, and the length of the period of apprenticeship varied with the different occupations.

Of course, too, while each member of the tribe had a field of specialization, he or she was usually versed in the rudiments of many crafts. One common factor in all vocational training however, was learning the particular religious ritual which accompanied each type of work.

Absolute and faithful obedience to all superiors was the keynote of the ancient Mexican educational system. Since all of the institutional education centered about the temple, the influence of the priesthood was paramount. It was thus within their power to mold the minds of the future leaders and followers of each successive generation.

The ancient Aztec was told under this complex theological and administrative machine, what he or she must think and feel in each relation and circumstance of life. A rigid, daily ceremonial, replete with minutiae, worked its knowledge into the child's hands, feet, head, and heart.

Unfortunately for the Aztecs, this acceptance of religious authoritarianism was to constitute an important factor after the Spanish Conquest, in the easy transition to accepting education from the hands of the Spanish priests, to the detriment and practical destruction of their own extraordinary cultural traditions.

So it was that in the fateful year of 1519, bearded men came from the East in small caravels. Armed with fierce weaponry, they plunged the throne of Montezuma into the lake of Mexico, and with it, the civilization of Anahuac.

The fall of the Aztec empire before the Spanish Conquistadors resulted in the loss of its art, its religion, its social structure, and its language—all that a people must maintain if they are to attain a racial destiny.

The development of the arts and sciences, and the growth of the communities of the ancient and magnificent Mexican empire came to an abrupt halt; and then began the gradual sinking and disintegration of a great people which lasted for more than four centuries.

It would be difficult indeed to find in history a more convincing example of the complete disaster that befell a people when stripped of its native culture.

978-0-595-48909-1
0-595-48909-5